DAILY DECADENCE

For Carrie!

Have Fun... I would.

xo

DAILY DECADENCE

The Art of Sensual Living

SHERRI DOBAY

Flying Archer Press, Calistoga, CA

For information about special discounts for bulk purchases, contact Flying Archer Press at info@daily-decadence.com

Printed in Canada
Cataloging-in-Publication Data
Dobay, Sherri
Daily Decadence The Art of Sensual Living
ISBN 978-0-9840457-0-9

For Mark

Acknowledgments

Thanks to everyone who helped make this labor of love a reality. I give endless gratitude for the inspiration of my Mom and Dad, the organization of Stephanie each day, the guidance of Jim, the magic of Cordelia's eyes and mind, the incredible photos by Greg, the sweetest support from Audrey, the style of Luke. Thanks also to John and his team, without whom I would not have had the guts to carry the project out, and to all my faithful tasters, who kept boisterous company in my kitchen. And to Mark, always at my side, with me and looking straight ahead.

If you really are who you really are, then you will live a life of beauty and truth and light.—Sherri Dobay

DAILY DECADENCE

Bockenhault 2000f, 2003
brian   Porcupine Ridge Syrah
Ⓝ pennyroyal, humidor, cigar
Ⓟ slightly pruny, smoked salmon,
    baked yam w/ brown sugar

Simon Pelt Syrah CA Ridge Creek Syrah '05
               pound cake
Ⓝ licqorice?tions & easter eggs
Ⓟ sassafras, ballet slipper/pink leather

Bonham Clateau Fombrauge St. Emilion
                              Tradition
Ⓝ quiet nose, wobbly-cherry stems
   almond? butter cookie
Ⓟ jasmin in finish, tannins

Sue Simon Grand Vindes Cotes du Rhone
              Gigondas 98
Ⓝ blueberry (sardiners underneath)
Ⓟ cherry tree bark, raspberry
                         snow cone

Limerick Lane 2001 Syrah
Ⓝ licorice   Collins Vineyard
Ⓟ ginger ale, white pepper (hungarian
                              barrels)

what price say you the syrah? B
you know Brian, I flipped a coin in my head
                         -John

Turnbull 99 tempranillo
Ⓝ thistles, earthy   "Napa Cabbville"
Ⓟ black cherry

Ramirez de Ganuza Rioja
Ⓝ sweet peas   '96.
Ⓟ black olives

Syrah? Resignac Vendanges 2001
Ⓝ bourbon, coffee, rubber, bordeaux
Ⓟ soft pepper, lots of fruit

SHERRI AND HER NOTEBOOKS

Every once in a while a book comes along that's so perfect for the times. *Daily Decadence* celebrates life the way we should live it—minute by minute, day by day, meal by meal, bite by bite, savoring each sip, exploring the nuances of love and pleasure, no matter where we are.

The first time I met its author, Sherri Dobay, we were at a summer dinner party together, seated outside on a deck at a friend's home in Alexander Valley. I immediately noticed that we shared a habit. We are both note-takers.

I carry an old standard-issue reporter's spiral notebook and scribble illegible reminders. Sherri had a fancier, moleskin notepad, and her memos to herself had what I call girl's pretty handwriting or pretty girl's handwriting.

As we came to know each other and shared a new circle of friends, I became more interested in Sherri and her notebook. It seemed as if we always met around lunches or dinners where wine bottles were one of the centers of attention. I finally asked her what she was writing in her notebook, the sort of nosy intrusion most would rebuff. Not so with Sherri. She was more than happy to share—at least most parts of it.

It was a hodgepodge of tasting notes, wine stains, random drawings, romantic interludes, horse sketches—whatever came to mind at an instant. That's the cool thing about taking notes. You capture a moment or a thought or an emotion, which makes it easier to return and revisit that frame of mind later on.

As I spent more time with Sherri, I realized what a special, talented, thoughtful and creative person she is. We share many passions connected to writing, food and wine, travel and adventure. When we talk about our lives and travels and experiences, Sherri always has her trusty moleskin and pen present.

I learned some things about her over time. She grew up in northeastern Ohio, on a horse farm. One thing that defined her childhood: playing outside with her sister, using their imaginations and making up their own games. Early on, even in the bleak winters and scraggly falls, Sherri found beauty. "In Ohio, after the flourish of fall, the color drains out of everything," she explained one day. "Once the winter starts, the landscape is a thousand shades of gray. A lot of people would be discouraged by that, but I found it beautiful in its own way."

She started keeping notes when she was 15, on Christmas Day when she was given a journal, "a little girly pink and purply thing with a lock, and I wish I had used the lock," she confides. For once her Mom read it, and learned of her secret late-night escapades with boys, she was grounded. But she still has that first journal.

There have always been horses in Sherri's life, and they have become a signature of her art. "People ask me why I always paint horses," she says. "I tell them that even when I draw people, they end up on the canvas as horses!"

Sherri's passion for cooking grew from childhood, spending time in the kitchen and watching her grandmother prepare meals. Her father, a hunter, taught her how to roast game outside on open fires.

At 18, Sherri headed to college, starting at Kent State University and finishing at Lake Erie College, an equestrian "all-girls horsey private school." In between, she took a year to live and travel in England, Ireland and France, and her love of extended travel was born. She kept her bags packed, and within a few years lived in Amsterdam, in the Netherlands, and Perugia, Italy, exploring both of those countries in depth.

Once graduated, and having lived in Europe, Sherri set her sights on the West Coast, especially Northern California. There she focused on her painting, while also falling in love with the region's wine culture in its multitude of facets.

As I write these thoughts, I keep coming back to Sherri's notebooks. Now numbering nearly 60 and collected in a variety of shapes and sizes, they brim with moments and musings that invigorate and inspire.

Wonder what's inside all those journals? Simply turn the page as the adventure begins. Join Sherri on the back seat of a motor scooter navigating the narrow roads of the Amalfi Coast, riding her horse

Bella at sunset out by the old redwood barn, nestled in front of a roaring fire sipping Champagne, or preparing a romantic dinner. Daily Decadence is playful, flirty, sexy and revealing in a way that inspires warmth and comfort. Enjoy!

—James Laube
Napa, Calif.
Jan. 1, 2012

INTRODUCTION

The time has come to redefine decadence. All around, there are fabulous things ready to indulge in if you simply stop, open your eyes and yourself to touch, taste, feel—celebrate—something each day. Very simply, this book is about inspiring you to include decadence in each day of your life. It comes in endless forms if you are aware.

At the winery where I live, I pass through the tasting room often and find myself stopping to say hello to blissed-out tasters. Over and over I hear the words, "I love this place. You're so lucky to live here! It's a paradise."

And I know—I love it as well. I definitely do not take it for granted. I pinch myself a lot. The guests are always saying (while swirling a taste of Petite Sirah) that this is their "annual vacation" and that they "only get a week or two" (insert wistful sigh here) and that the day after tomorrow it's back to the grind again. I have thought about this perspective at length, about what it means in the big picture. The world is on the fast track to efficiency (and ulcers) thanks to technology and the resulting ability to work 24/7. It's no surprise that it drains us and leaves us empty, unfulfilled and lost as we lose the ability to pause and enjoy life on a daily basis.

Wine is a slow thing. In wine country, we're in tune with the seasons, close to nature and her nuances because we are awake and aware and listening. Why? We have to be. It's what wine is all about. It starts in the vineyard, one morning at a time. We celebrate a lot, often just so we can open a bottle and see how our latest release is doing. We don't need much prompting or preparation to invite in a little decadence. I believe that this is what visitors feel when they come here. What they don't realize is that this sense of calm and lusciousness can apply to anyone, anywhere. No winery required. You can find yourself living decadently right now where you are with a simple shift in attitude, a more sensitive ability to observe and a conscious effort to invite even five minutes of celebration into your packed day.

You could say this simple way of life is in my blood from growing up on a horse farm. I learned all about slow as a little girl in the middle of nowhere, and fell in love with it. I milked cows, baled hay and spent hours contemplating life from the back of my pony. Born an artist, I took it upon myself to cultivate a taste for decadence with my eyes and ears wide open. By working three jobs I sent myself to school and was able to spend many years of my life traveling and learning about artists and their loves and lives in Italy, the Netherlands, France, England and Greece. Because of hard work and respect I knew what gifts glittered all around me, and faithfully recorded details about them in books, year after year, filling up creamy blank pages with drawings and words. I fell in love with observation. The process of capturing these details on paper created an awareness in me that touched all of my senses. I described what I saw from the train I rode as it snaked from station to screaming station all over Europe under the cold snow. I wrote about the sensual feel of a fistful of horsehair clutched in my hand at the age of 16 while my pony raced across an open field, a boy holding my waist tightly from behind. I scribbled about the earthy taste of ultra local cheeses at an out-of-the-way hotel restaurant one balmy June night in the north of Italy. I kept notes on the sweet scent of crush in the Napa Valley and the sound of the Pacific crashing softly as a lover's breath in my ear. I carried my notebooks to dinners and wine events, collecting tasting notes like pressed flowers among the pages. I learned that tuning in to the senses is a gift. When you do, the world comes alive, and you are nowhere else but in that moment, living it to the fullest. This is true decadence.

Now these diaries and sketchbooks holding two-and-a-half decades of stories, wine tasting notes, love letters and the most intimate details of my wild and wide-awake life are spread about me. It is from them that I have plucked the juiciest (well, almost) bits for you, with the hope that you as well will cultivate a taste for slowing down, looking around, breathing deep and finding true indulgence right where you sit this minute.

Within the pages of this book I hope you will find many things to inspire you to add a bit of indulgence into every day, that my stories and letters, horse tales and painting excursions, wine notes and recipes from my kitchen and the kitchens of my friends and family offer insight for living a luscious life each day, no matter how busy you are.

This is not a traditional cookbook, and I am in no way a professional in the culinary realm, but I do eat several times a day, as I am sure you do as well. Here you will find real, and usually simple, delicious recipes. The stories in this book are followed by recipes inspired by the message or the characters told of. For me, memory is closely linked to the sensual side of life. It's easy to remember sweet moments which included a meal or something cooking in the background. It's how the simple smell of the creamy white flesh of a perfectly baked potato conjures my mother's dimly lit table, a cool chunk of yellow butter sliding apart in that salted fluff while Junebugs buzzed just outside the screen door, whispering with the evening breeze and summer sunset. Powerfully simple food.

My experience in the Napa Valley wine country has given me education and insight into the world of winegrowing (not to mention invitations to fabulous dinners and parties). Napa Valley is a taster's paradise—and yet I have learned that the best food is simple and clean, prepared with passion and high quality local ingredients that shine next to our wines. Don't be surprised at the simplicity of the recipe collection here. To me, decadence is the ability to literally throw something together and tuck it in the oven while you relax with someone important to you, or in blissful peace all alone, as it bubbles to perfection on its own. The suggestions are approachable, fun and prepared with basic ingredients you may have in your pantry right now. I also include wine pairing ideas and tasting notes, which I hope invite you to indulge in an exploration of wine. Trust yourself and experiment with your tongue. After all, she knows you best!

This book found you because it is time for you to begin slipping a bit of decadence into your days. Remember, a little bit of naughty can be very nice. While not necessarily that kind of naughty (which, incidentally, is encouraged), the kind of naughty I'm talking about is the type we normally reserve for special occasions—like the weekend or that annual vacation. Have you noticed that while we are busy each day rushing from deadline to deadline, hoping to reach the big prize at the end, the world keeps right on turning? Suddenly, exhausted, you stop for a breath and realize that six years have slid by unnoticed, without so much as a postcard from yourself to remind you where you've been! It's time to add some tiny treat, some little luxury, some small something special—into each day of your own amazing life. Don't save up for an annual opportunity to take care of yourself; it may be too late. You deserve decadence every day—and in these pages I hope you find real ways to invite it in.

In our crazy-busy lives, even a little luxury goes a long way. You won't believe how easy it really is. Slow down, breath in and notice the world around you with its endless beauty, waiting to dazzle you!

DISCOVERING DECADENCE

It has been my experience that the process of awakening to a discovery can take two distinct speeds: either slow, like the quiet emergence of the first whispery green spring shoots on the bare vines at bud break, or all at once in a rush, like the flying sensation that is the uplifting transition of riding from trot to canter on a strong mare. Each of these speeds offers its own brand of decadence. The one, voluptuous and gradual, allowing time for luscious digestion. The other a swift, thrilling, transcendent departure.

Inspiration From My Notes: Four Days In June; Day One

Now I understand that this is what is supposed to be happening to me. All alone now at a gorgeous new resort in the first stages of being built here in Carneros, in the late afternoon sun and waiting my turn at the hot soaking tub. I am enjoying myself very much. The sky is cerulean, the grass a lush green. Swallows dip and swirl above my head. Vineyards stretch out to the right of me as far as I can see. They are beautiful and emerald and rich. The hills beyond that, with their bushy low oaks, create Tuscan shadows on the golden straw grass. I picked a bit of lavender and it is keeping me company—a small purple bud of a piece.

My life has taken this very interesting turn. I am suddenly and unexpectedly quite happy. I am letting go of fear and stress, though that in itself is a little scary. Who am I? Who am I if I don't have worries? But things are different now, today, in this thin, warm evening, which begs me to unfurl into it like new sheets tossed with a flick of the wrist across a cool, wide bed. I'm ready to let go.

Pale blue sky—long, straw-colored hills rolling away from me, the green lines of the vineyards, the soft push of warm winds, the salty water from the clear pool on my lips, the constant sun warming me everywhere, finally! The moon three-quarters full rising early in a pale blue sky, the scent of blood orange in the bath, warm red tiles under my feet. Half-made paintings spread around me, open, inviting me in, to taste again the source, the divine source, finding mine. As ever.

I feel like I have been given a gift and the permission to make my very own charmed reality. Realize that you are already here. Enjoy it. Stop searching for the rainbow—look up, it shines above your head! From now on: less worry, less angst, less fear, more painting, more pleasure more love, more lightness.

Did you ever have one of those days, nights, times that just seemed to define decadence for you? Remember the way you felt then? The suspension of time, the true melting into the world around you in perfect calmness? Go back to that moment in your life. See if you can write it down now. Don't leave out details, no one will read this but you (toss it in the fireplace afterward if you want to). Breathe deeply and invite more moments like this into your world as of now.

Everyday Indulgence: Lobster & Eggs Benedict

This is the perfect dish to make if you've had a decadently adventurous night and went to bed but not to sleep. It's also a fabulous breakfast for dinner if you want to raise an eyebrow or something more. It wouldn't hurt to pop that bottle of vintage Champagne you've been holding onto, as this rich dish wants a touch of sparkle to complete the package.

Ingredients

2 large lobster tails, deveined

4 postage stamp–sized pats of butter, plus 4 tablespoons

Coarse salt and fresh pepper

4 fresh eggs for poaching

2 English muffins

4 cups fresh spinach

Hollandaise Sauce

1 stick salted butter

4 egg yolks

1 teaspoon water

Fresh juice of ½ of lemon

Paprika

Coarse salt

Ground white pepper

Prepare a bucket of ice. Add 2 cups cold water. Insert a good bottle of Champagne, and set to the side. While I'm a fan of nudity, I do not advise cooking that way, so if you're still wearing only a portion of what you went out in last night, go find yourself an apron. Safety first. While you're rummaging around, turn up the Ella Fitzgerald you have playing in the other room.

Put a pot on to boil. This is for your eggs, so just enough water to cover four of them is plenty. While the water comes to a boil, prepare the lobster.

Set the oven to broil. Using kitchen scissors, carefully snip down either edge of the belly side of the tails until you can unzip the meat in one voluptuous chunk. I like to use the empty shells as little pedestals upon which to broil the meat. Place each tail shell on a baking sheet, and drape the meat over the top. Place two stamps of butter on each tail, then salt and pepper to taste. Put the lobster under the hot broiler. Mind the time, as this meat cooks fast. You will need to check it and turn it over after just 3 minutes. Six minutes total is about all it will need. Overcooked lobster is a buzzkill at best, a deal breaker at worst. Remove the cooked tails and let them rest. Turn the broiler off, and set the oven to 250 ° F.

In preparation for the English muffins (and the spinach), melt 4 tablespoons butter over medium heat in a large sauté pan. While this is melting, you can start your eggs. Turn the boiling water down to a simmer, and carefully drop 4 freshly cracked eggs one at a time into the water. "How's that Champagne chilling down?" Hopefully that hint produces a large popping sound in your near future. (Ah yes, the joys of cooking are many.) Cook your eggs in the simmering water until the white is firm and the yolk is still soft, nudging them around to keep them a bit separate and off the bottom of the pan. The eggs will take about 3 minutes to cook. Meanwhile, slice the English muffins and dredge them in the now-melted butter in the pan next door. Place the muffins on a baking sheet and tuck into your warmed oven to crisp them up. The eggs will be ready to go now. Remove them from the cooking water, reserving it to rewarm them later. Another good trick is to have a cool water bath ready to receive the poached eggs. Simply place the soft cooked eggs into the chilly water, and the cooking will stop. Now you can set them aside and make the Hollandaise sauce.

Have a sip of Champagne. While this sauce does require your attention, it is not as difficult as you might think. In a bowl, melt a whole stick of butter in your microwave. In a medium saucepan, combine 4 egg yolks and about a teaspoon of water. Over medium heat, whisk the yolks until frothy and light. I regulate my heat even further by hovering the pan a bit above the medium flame, moving it closer or farther away to keep it at the correct temperature. You want the pan very warm but not so warm that you end up with scrambled eggs instead of Hollandaise sauce. A good test for the proper temperature is to check if you can lightly touch the bottom of the pan—if it is too hot to touch, your heat is too high. While you whisk, slowly add the butter to the frothy eggs, about a tablespoon at a time. Stay on top of the heat. After the butter is incorporated, and the sauce thickens again, add the juice of half of one lemon. Continue stirring this in, adding salt and white pepper to taste. If you like an extra kick, a few shakes of Tabasco are completely appropriate. Now, set the sauce aside, and start your assembly.

Pull the crisped English muffins from the oven. Slice the lobster into ½-inch thick medallions and arrange them on top of the English muffins. Top the lobster meat with a tablespoon or so of Hollandaise sauce, and return the dish to the oven. Place the poached eggs back into the warm water bath on the stovetop for about 30 seconds to awaken them. Using a slotted spoon and a towel to catch the extra water, remove the eggs from the warm bath, and position them on top of the lobster-stacked muffins. Top each serving with more sauce, and return to the oven to warm for a few moments more.

In the large sauté pan where you melted your butter earlier, pile in the fresh spinach. Over medium heat, wilt the spinach down just slightly, salting and peppering a little as you go. Many of my friends swear by nutmeg; if you feel so moved, pinch in a bit. Tossing, tossing until it gives.

Turn the oven off, and pull out the piping hot lobster muffins. Plate them with love, side them with spinach, and top with a flick of paprika. Grab the Champagne bucket and get to the table. Then, slow down. Savor this dish. Isn't it a lovely day? You may find that all of those egg baths and bubbles have inspired you. Start a tub, tie up your hair. It is going to be one of those mornings. Are you ready? Of course you are.

My Perfect Pairing: Dom Pérignon 1990

From my notes: *Potato chip with crème fraîche and caviar at Betsy's house, kettle corn nose, mushrooms and cream soda, roasted chestnuts, croissants and almond paste. Oh my how I love this*

Inspiration From My Notes: The Power Of A Roasted Carrot

It's timeless. When we're together, we step off the planet.

In front of the fire now and just made love with every cell in my body. Physical, emotional, beautiful and nice. I love this man with all that I am. I hope he marries me someday. I may go away with him this weekend. It's a start.

... His arms, the slant of his body when he's above me. The way he turns in on me and envelops me in public. How he laughs. His stories, all of them. His courage, his tenacity.

Am I happy, really happy for the first time in my life? Am I truly living love for the first time in my life? Have I tasted a more delicious roasted carrot, ever? My life is so very blessed these days—so much more alive and real. And, so strange at the same time, balance is there. I feel taken care of but not controlled. Loved but not smothered, guided but not led. It is amazing and I am living it wide awake.

This entry followed a perfectly roasted chicken and a fireside picnic. Never underestimate the power of simply being present.

Everyday Indulgence: Perfectly Roasted Chicken

The argument could be made that a nicely roasted chicken is a good answer to a lot of problems, and I would have to agree. My question is, how can something that is so good be so easy to make? Not only is the first version of it perfect, this dish can go on and on if you are so inclined. Chicken livers wrapped in bacon, chicken salad, chicken soup, and you even get to make a wish at the end! You can roast a chicken any time of the day. I usually roast mine after lunch unless I want to make (The Best) Chicken Soup (Ever), in which case I will make it in the morning and let it slow roast for several hours.

Now a word of advice here. I suggest you have company for this dinner, as it is an aphrodisiac. Don't believe me? Read my Ode to a Perfectly Roasted Chicken, a love poem, which follows. Yes, I actually wrote this. So here it is. You may want to take a deep breath now.

Ingredients

Whole organic roasting chicken	1 or 2 onions, any of red, yellow, white
Olive oil	
1 bulb garlic, cloved and peeled as needed	Redskin potatoes
	Carrots
Coarse salt and fresh pepper	Handful of each of rosemary, thyme, oregano*
1 whole lemon	

Is this in your garden?

To make this amazing creation, rinse the chicken and pat her dry. Massage her with olive oil and salt and pepper. Really put the love in that rub (that's the secret ingredient)! Next, press the garlic, and rub the garlic press and all right on top of her oily salty skin. Stuffing means a million options, but this is a simple chicken: stuff the body cavity with a handful of fresh rosemary, a bunch of thyme, some oregano, a whole lemon that has first been rolled hard on the counter to release its oils, a few cloves of garlic sliced simply in half and some good coarse salt and pepper.

Let the chicken rest. Meanwhile, chop the onion, potatoes and some more garlic. Peel the carrots so they are pretty (important). Toss the potatoes and carrots in a big bowl with some olive oil, rosemary, salt and pepper and the onions. Arrange all of this in a bed on a baking sheet if you plan to use a little rack to roast the bird on, or in a big casserole dish if you like to let everything get juicy together. This seems to be a personal preference. I go both ways if you know what I mean. You can do the bird breast up or down, again, your call. Slip that beautiful creation into the oven at about 350° F for at least 2 ½ hours. You can turn it down and roast at 250° F for longer as well. All you need is a simple salad and a nice bottle of anything from Champagne to Cabernet to complete your evening of bliss. And I do mean bliss. You may want to light the fire before dinner. I'm serious. Read the following letter.

Love Letters: Ode To A Perfectly Roasted Chicken

This is a real letter I gave to a lover after this magical chicken once. I was running late and he had to leave before we could eat, so I dined alone. He returned later that evening.

Dearest,

Perhaps a woman, at one time in your life, wrote you a card about a wonderful meeting, or a spectacular night of rollicking lovemaking, or even about a serious conversation spoken among beautiful dunes during a long and revealing walk on some seashore. I am writing to you tonight about a perfectly roasted chicken. Deep inside its luscious flesh, I am communing with all that is right in the universe. Sweet, tender roasted carrots, perfectly salted, and do I taste a shiver of cayenne, the spice mixed perfectly with the decadent juices of the meat? The potatoes try to keep me grounded but fail—their earthiness only lending to the deep connection I feel with each naughty bite to the base, the beginning, the essence of Creation. The peas, playful, flirt with me to crunch on them, their oniony-slippery outsides sleek with something slidy—could it be butter? Or the just the touch of you? But it is the chicken itself that drives me to the edge, pushes me back, then pulls again with a sticky, salty taste in one perfect bite—mmm—and the juices drench my lips and chin, and I sit alone, trembling, until your return, when I should hope you lick it off and share in its divinity with me.

All my love.

My Perfect Pairing: Carter Cellars Cabernet Sauvignon Fortuna Block

From my notes: *Raspberry strudel sitting on a saddle. Beehives and marmalade, structured briary berries, anise, dry cedar and the glaze on duck breast. Plus all those things I remember from before ...*

Inspiration From My Notes: Dawn Comes Late Sometimes

It was the clearest blue I had ever seen, the sky that day. The air was just chilly enough. The sunshine danced around us while we clipped down the dirt road on that October afternoon. My buckskin pony shook her head at me, tugging lightly at the bit. She wanted to trot faster. I sank deep to slow her down, even though we were on the way to my crush's house. I wanted that perfect fall day to stretch and go on forever. I was fourteen. I laid my head back and drank in the sky—tree branches slicing the blue and cadmium autumn leaves into a kaleidoscope of stained glass above us. I can still feel the reins in my hand now, and the saddle under me, full of dancing pony.

A mile later, off went the saddle and up came the boy, sitting behind me, bareback, one arm lightly wrapped around my waist and the other resting on my buckskin's warm rump, his pelvis pressed firmly against mine. We wound through the trees to the big lake—and everywhere else—that day. But the sun goes down fast in the fall, and bright days trick you into thinking the long twilights of summer are still hanging on. In fact, they can even make you stay out late and miss curfew, which everyone knows is right at dusk.

The temptation of that ride was too great to resist. We crested a little hill to watch the molten sun slip below the tree line. I tied the reins together and dropped them against the neck of my horse. While we were both still astride her big warm back, I spun completely around to face the boy. We sat like that for a long time, my legs draped over his, his legs wrapped around her, while she buried her head in the long grass that curled up and touched the heels of our boots. My first threesome. I leaned in, too afraid to kiss him, and simply rested my head in the warm space between the collar of his jean jacket and his heavenly jawbone. The touch of his neck against my forehead was a thousand kisses to me. As the sun sank down, I memorized the song of the wind, his breath and the soft sound of my mare slowly eating grass. And I replayed it again and again every day after that, which I spent at home—grounded for returning to the dimly lit barn too late that night. Worth it.

Decadence can come at a price, but often the gain outweighs the loss. Drop the reins.

Everyday Indulgence: Mushroom And Love Risotto

I once made a huge pot of risotto while taking recipe direction over the phone from a faraway lover. While he instructed blindly into my ear, I toiled. His voice was steady and soothing, but I could feel that something was terribly wrong. I had somehow doubled the rice proportion, and even though I thought I was following along just fine, I had failed to add enough liquid to the recipe. He told me that there would be much laborious stirring involved, and so I took him quite literally and continued to stir and stir and stir the stiff mass.

"Is it supposed to be thick?" I asked as a cramp developed in my left forearm. "Oh yes!" he cooed into the phone, uncomfortably squeezed between my shoulder and cheek. "Is it supposed to need a lot of stirring?" I questioned, as I watched the ball of paste grow, trying to keep it from sticking to the bottom of the pan. "Yes lots of stirring!" he said simply, proving that everything is relative. "You have to make love to risotto. Keep up the touching. It takes time."

At this point the rice was the consistency of concrete mixed with glue, not a creamy, sensual risotto. I must have stirred that cementlike glob for an hour, my own sweat salting the pot in an act of accomplishment devoted only to my absent love. Later, we made this recipe side by side, with pale Champagne dancing in our touching glasses and the right amount of stock. Amazing! It was then I laughed at my miscalculation and myself. I smiled at the ease with which love could be made to risotto, my old wooden spoon gliding effortlessly around the pot, beckoning me to touch its silky smoothness all over, over and over again.

Ingredients

3 cups sliced cremini mushrooms	Coarse salt and fresh pepper
1 cup arborio rice	¼ cup dry vermouth
1 cup diced onion	6 cups chicken stock (use 3 cubes of bouillon for this stock)
4 tablespoons butter	
3 cloves of garlic, pressed	2 cups grated hard cheese (Parmigiano is good)
4 tablespoons olive oil	Your favorite wooden spoon

Risotto is a lovely way to end a stressful week and kick off a relaxing weekend. The more frazzled you are, the better. Let the risotto comfort and soothe you, starting with its sensual preparation. I like a little Charlie Parker in the background and at least six candles lighting my way.

Melt 4 tablespoons butter in deep soup pot. With the heat set on medium, slide in the diced onion, garlic and salt and pepper. Cook until the onions are translucent and tender, and the flavors start to blend. While the onions are cooking, heat your stock in a separate saucepan over medium heat. It is very important to have the stock ready and to keep it hot, but not boiling.

Once the onions have surrendered to the cause, add 4 tablespoons olive oil and the rice. Using your favorite wooden spoon, stir to evenly coat each rice kernel with your love. Continue stirring during the whole next song. Let go of the tensions of the week; give yourself up in that deep warm pot that now smells just about like I imagine and hope that heaven does. After the rice is well-coated with everything, add the vermouth, and stir some more. After this foreplay, add about 2 cups stock, and stir again. At this point, she can simmer and think about things while you work on the mushrooms. As her liquid reduces, keep replenishing cup-by-cup, and stirring until the rice is cooked. Just keep an eye on things, and your spoon nearby.

In a large sauté pan, start the mushrooms. Salt them well; add nothing else. Over medium heat they will sweat their own nectar soon. Let them cook down, adding just a bit more salt if needed to taste, and maybe a twist of pepper. After the mushrooms are reduced a bit, add a chunk of butter to richen them up even more, and shut off the heat. Now is a good time to grate your Parmigiano-Reggiano and enjoy a little wine. After this, test the rice for doneness. The kernels should be the consistency of warm chestnuts—soft but not mushy and with a resilient texture. Blend two-thirds of the sautéed mushrooms into the creamy risotto along with most of the grated cheese. Add a splash of olive oil to the remaining mushrooms, and crisp them up a bit in the sauté pan. Ladle out plates of risotto and top with crispy mushrooms and a thoughtful toss of cheese. Sit down in the candlelight and savor the love.

My Perfect Pairing: Château Mouton Rothschild

From my notes: *Super-rich violets, a floral explosion, dried lavender and pony fur, coffee pots and warm, earthy nuts, my favorite*

Love Letters: The Awakening

For a time I wrote letters to a man I had only met in person for a few moments at a party, near a roaring fire on a cold night, right around midnight. The exchange of letters was innocent of flesh but was doubtlessly decadence of the pen. It awakened in me words long left silent and waiting for their moment. It was finally time to work them out. Now some of those words have found their way into this book.

Hello …

You are a great pen pal. I wrote to a girl in Germany from fifth to eighth grade and even though she drew elephants on every letter she sent, you are better.

Yes, there is something incredible about the notes: the power to inspire. I think we were meant to have this strange chapter (or do you always start writing wonder-full and interesting notes to girls you meet at parties for five minutes?), so in spite of the thinnish ice upon which I stand, I will keep typing.

I grew up in arctic winters (actually the Midwest, lovely seasons). Once, under a full moon at 3 a.m., in a strange house (we had been at a party there), my father woke me to go for a walk in the moonlight. He took me to a giant frozen reservoir. We walked all over the glassy surface of that still water, pale blue in the moon's gaze. The trees were draped in soft snow. Our dog was a black shadow slipping through the night around us.

We stayed for a long time. It was completely magical. I will never forget it. I trusted my father and held his leathery hand and drank it all in. I was twelve.

In later years, he would admit that it might have been dangerous: the time of night; no one knew where we were; the ice could have given at any time. But he said that he trusted the instincts of our dog, and that as long as she was trotting around without worry, we could too.

That memory is one of my favorite tastes of danger. It was exquisite. So I have learned to trust my instincts and follow adventures. Or write to handsome men with nice calves who send me romantic notes and bottles of wine.

I opened the '99. I thought it would be fun to start in the middle. Speaking of the middle, have a really nice Wednesday. Tomorrow is my birthday. I am celebrating all week. Tonight, the '98?

Best best thoughts.

Taking risks that push you into new territory may seem dangerous when you are unsure of the outcome.

What's waiting may just delight you in spite of yourself. Let your instincts guide you, they will not let you down. What can you hand over to your gut to decide right now? Whether you are creating or cooking or working with a new client, the end result will taste better and not give you a tummy ache.

Everyday Indulgence: Venison Steaks On The Fire With Roasted Rosemary Potatoes

My father loves to have meals over open fires outside. Any little excuse will do, and the time of year is irrelevant. Once inspired, he crafts a stack of squaw wood and tinder, careful as a nuthatch making a nest, as the starting point of his great fire. He builds them slow and well and strong. The preparation allows him to sit back and relax as they burn long and hot later. This is important for the roasting of the meat. Perhaps it is the meat that he really loves. A hunter all his life, known for patiently waiting endless hours 30 feet up an oak tree in the frozen air stalking his prey, he is dedicated to the process and grateful for the results. We grew up eating game of all sorts, from black bear to mallard duck, often prepared by him. One of my favorites is his simple venison steaks, best shared in a snow camp, with mittens off and breath steaming in puffs, in some center of a still forest of black, bare-branched trees. The warm circle around the radius of the fire was a safe and comfortable place to relax and have dinner in your snowsuit, even lick buttery steak juice from your fingers. A few inches away, and the bite of winter won.

Ingredients

Carefully butchered wild venison back strap (the silverback lining and all fat removed), cut into ¾ to 1-inch thick medallions, rinsed well and patted dry

Coarse salt and fresh pepper

2 cloves garlic, pressed, plus 2 whole cloves thinly sliced

Onion, sliced

Paprika

Olive oil (for brushing)

Butter, at least 1 stick, cold

6 to 8 small to medium Idaho potatoes, or small yams

Sprigs of rosemary or dried rosemary

To prepare the medallions, brush the clean meat lightly with olive oil, then rub with the pressed garlic. Season the steaks on both sides with salt, pepper and a touch of paprika. Layer the medallions on top of a generous slice of onion, and arrange the stacks on wax paper. Salt and pepper them again. The meat can marinate this way for up to one whole day.

The potatoes may also be prepared ahead. Slice a pocket into each potato, and season inside the slice with lots of fresh pepper and a good sprinkle of salt. Add thinly sliced garlic, a sprig of fresh rosemary (or a few shakes of the dried version), and a chunk of butter. Place the potatoes on foil and fold the sides up. When you have pulled the sides up in a little bowl shape, douse the potatoes with about a tablespoon of cold water, then seal everything tightly inside the foil wrap.

On your campfire night, about an hour before sunset, build a fire and watch it burn, preparing a glowing bed of very hot coals. Enjoy the stillness of the forest around you, or the hush of your neighborhood if you are working on a patio grill just past your kitchen door.

Early on, place your foil-wrapped potatoes around the edges of the fire, turning them often and moving them in towards the heat as it starts to tame. If you are grilling on the patio, place them on the rack and turn every 10 minutes or so. Luxuriate in the snow-stilled dark, letting it wrap like a blanket close around you and your glowing fire. As this fire preparation will take about 45 minutes to an hour, keep some 1-inch split pieces of firewood nearby, adding them as needed to keep the heat high but the flames under control.

On an open fire, the venison preparation is most simple using a meat-grilling basket. When you have told a few stories and the coals finally glow hot, oil the grill basket with olive oil, and place the medallions inside, discarding the onions. Place the grill basket on top of a grate placed above the fire. Watch the meat carefully now, this is not the time to become distracted by the rising moon or the restless coyotes in the brush over there. When the meat sizzles, as it will on a hot fire after just a few minutes, flip the basket over and continue to cook evenly. After 5 to 8 minutes, open the grill basket and rub both sides of the meat with a cold stick of butter. Continue to watch the meat, rub with butter, and turn it again. Venison is lean: Butter is your friend and overcooking is your enemy. At 10 minutes cooking time, test a steak for doneness.

Move the fire grate higher, away from the coals but still in the warm zone, and let the meat rest here. The rosemary potatoes should be baked through now. Pull them out of the coals and open up the foil, being careful of their warm, puffy steam. You will find their foil makes a perfect, simple plate upon which to eat this entire meal, and using your fingers is quite acceptable.

My Perfect Pairing: Château Margaux

From my notes: *Chocolate almonds, delicious, extraordinary, yes it's true what they say of Margaux, lilac and dried dusty herbs ... pure perfume in a glass*

DIVINE DECADENCE

Routine yet unexpected communion with the other side has been an inevitable part of my sensualist life. Since I was a little girl catching fireflies in our big, pony pasture at dusk, tapping into the energetic magic of the universe has been a favorite pastime of mine. A bug that lights up? And it allows me to capture it for a moment, hold it in my hands? And sometimes if I am very still it even lands on my warm T-shirt on its own? Pure magic. When you allow yourself permission to really see with your whole being, worlds blossom in front of you, and portals open and beckon that you never before imagined, often on the simplest plane. Show up. Look around. For me, the moon is often a handy accomplice.

Inspiration From My Notes: The Other Bud Break

There is a place in the Alexander Valley that I think of as the entry to my own personal heaven. The first time I went to the wine country of Napa I drove alone on the road from Geyserville to Calistoga, Highway 128, with my breath caught in my throat at the scenery that surrounded me around each bend. On this very warm early spring day, I rounded a curve and out stretched in front of me a million cherry blossoms. Lining each side of the thoroughfare as far as I could see were crimson-barked trees, exploding with white and pink flowers. It was like falling into a painting that went on for miles, and I was driving right down the center of it. I could not believe it was real. But it was, and it is. I have driven that road about 400 times since then. And each year, just when winter starts to erase my memory of what they look like in bloom, the trees hear the song of spring once more and explode with the colors of love.

Caught in a dull spot? Put fresh flowers on your table as a reminder to choose to dedicate yourself to your own personal slice of renewal whenever you need it.

Everyday Indulgence: The Ultimate Caesar Salad

Once, after a long day of bottling at the winery, we made the most delicious Caesar salad for the entire bottling crew. My love had promised a simple meal for the folks who came out and helped us that day. He served this salad alongside New York strip steaks off the grill. What impressed me most was his ability to expand the recipe to cover 16 people. We had to use a washtub, and two sets of arms up to our elbows to perform the mixing. He would not rest until each of the whole romaine leaves was perfectly coated with his homemade dressing and freshly grated cheese, and fortified with crunchy, flavorful, made-from-scratch croutons (absolutely essential). I was very relieved that we had enough steak knives to go around.

Ingredients

Full head of romaine lettuce	5 tablespoons olive oil
1 egg, coddled in the shell	Juice of 1 lemon
Freshly grated Parmigiano cheese, about ½ cup per head of lettuce	Dijon mustard
	2 to 3 cloves garlic
Worcestershire sauce	For the croutons: Good chunky, seedy, whole-grain bakery bread, cubed roughly
Coarse salt and fresh pepper	
Anchovies, from a tin, chopped	

If you have your own garden, try growing romaine. It is easy, and a homegrown head always tastes nuttier than one from a store. Wide, bright blue skies swept free of clouds and the clear songs of M. Ward set the scene for this meal and its preparation. The hardest part about putting this together is timing the coddled egg outside on the grill. Drag a pretty tablecloth and some mismatched place settings out to your patio, and set to work there.

First, in a large sauté pan, which will also be used for making your croutons soon, add enough water to cover an egg, and bring to a boil. Place a whole egg in the boiling water in for 30 seconds, then remove, and set egg aside to rest until you are ready to make your dressing.

Empty the water and dry the pan, to make the croutons. Now, I have never met a crouton I didn't like but this version blows my mind, as sometimes I like my decadence on the wholesome side if you know what I mean. Coat the bottom of the large sauté pan with 2 to 3 tablespoons of olive oil and while it is warming to medium, add minced garlic. Once the garlic is starting to crisp, add in those neat square pillows of cubed brown bread and let them do what they do best: suck up flavor like mad. With the heat on medium, crisp up the croutons on all sides, adding salt and pepper while you do it. Once they are golden brown, take them off the heat, but leave them in the pan to keep them slightly warm.

It is now that you may want to sit for a second with friends and admire the mountains and watch the birds dip in the olive trees and tell a few stories while you have a glass of chilly Sauvignon Blanc, and maybe, yes, maybe test those warm croutons to make sure they're OK. It's just an idea. Thus fortified, you will be ready to make the dressing.

In a bowl, whisk together the cracked coddled egg, the remaining 2 to 3 tablespoons olive oil, dash of mustard, chopped anchovies, garlic, Worcestershire sauce, lemon juice, salt and pepper. Whisk just long enough to froth it slightly. Drench over full-leaf romaine, crisped with a cool shower in the sink and a quick chill in the fridge, sitting refreshed in a nearby washtub. Make sure you coat each leaf evenly, and add in most of the grated cheese and all of the croutons. Plate the salad in generous green hills, sprinkle with more shredded Parmigiano from the old Italian grater your mother used, and top with the best croutons on planet Earth. Raise up your glass and toast to your health, happiness and those you hold dear, near and far (and to another vintage of wine safely in bottle).

My Perfect Pairing: Kathryn Hall Sauvignon Blanc

From my notes: *Pear, sea grass, sea breezy saltiness on creamy cheese; is that brie? Cool acid like a ripe green apple, lovely balance making my mouth water*

Inspiration From My Notes: Fathers and Daughters, Green Grass and Full Moons

My sister got married in the state of New York on a hot afternoon one August. This was the most casual affair, with no rehearsal dinner and no plan other than to walk out to the middle of an endless, cropped green field and stop by a special rock where the vows would be exchanged. The day was delicious. We wore sundresses. The first touch of fall teased the trees with color, but the day was warm. Eating and drinking and dancing followed under the swoop of an enormous white marquis. While I watched a boisterous bocce game, the voice of Dean Martin began to croon in the distance. I turned to my dad and asked him to dance. Suddenly shy, he said he didn't know how. I said, 'That's OK, I'll lead, I'll teach you.' We did a simple step and swirled around and laughed, and he was so GOOD! I enjoyed it so much. And others noticed as well how special the moment was. My sister's new father-in-law turned to my own lover who stood watching and said, "That's what this is all about. That's why I mowed this whole big field. This is it." (My love tried not to cry then, or later when he recounted this to me. I was not so strong.)

That evening ended with my father and my sister arm in arm as we all walked back to the house in the distance. "See that moon?" he leaned into her ear and said quietly, looking up at the ripe, light circle in the night sky. "That's a lover's moon." My bride-sister gazed up at it with him, in her white sundress now grass-stained from exhilarated dancing, and the moonlight reflected in their eyes, glistening. Then and there, I swear I almost died from the tenderness of it all.

Often decadence is just deep green grass. Isn't it time to take off your shoes? No wedding needed.

Everyday Indulgence: Slow-Roasted Pork Shoulder With Fresh Sage and Spice Rub

This is a fun dish to make, but like even a simple wedding, it takes a bit of planning. Marinate the meat for at least a day (or as long as a few). Don't cheat yourself and shorten this ritual. Now and then, tasty meat takes time.

Ingredients

1 boneless pork shoulder, about 4 pounds

1 tablespoon black peppercorns

1 tablespoon cinnamon

2 tablespoons brown sugar or turbinado sugar

3 cloves of garlic, chopped coarsely

Half an onion, or 1 large shallot, chopped coarsely

3 tablespoons chopped fresh sage

Chunky salt

¼ cup olive oil

Chunky Apple Fig Chutney (see recipe below)

Day one: Pick out a pretty pork shoulder from the nice meat man at the shop. On your way home, think about which three of your dearest friends you want to have over in the next few days to eat delicious pork roast.

Back at the ranch, get ready to rub! Toss the peppercorns and a dash of cinnamon (reserve the rest for the rub mix) into a small frying pan and heat over medium heat for a little while, releasing the oil in the pepper and coating it with cinnamon. Once their scent reaches your nose, turn the heat off and set the pan aside to cool. Untie the shoulder if it is tied up, rinse the pork in cold water and pat it dry. Put the cooled peppercorns, remaining cinnamon, sugar, chopped garlic, onion or shallot, sage and salt in a food processor. I have a little one that is really handy and easy to clean that I use all the time. Grind these ingredients into a coarse paste, then add half the oil, pulse a few times, and then add the rest of the oil, mixing everything until well-combined but still a little chunky.

Rub the mixture all over the pork shoulder, put the meat in a plastic bag and refrigerate for at least a day. Two or three days is even better (plus, it will give you time to make your dinner plans and some flexibility, too). For every day in the fridge, move the pork around in the bag a little and turn the meat over.

When your dinner plans are set and you're ready to cook the shoulder, pull it out of the fridge a couple of hours before cooking. You are going to cook the pork for about an hour and a half, then you will need to let it rest a few minutes before cutting, so plan accordingly. Preheat the oven to 450° F. Make a nice solid bundle of your pork with some strong kitchen twine; place the shoulder into a heavy roasting pan and pop it into the oven, uncovered. After about 15 minutes at 450° F, lower the temperature to 350° F and continue to roast the pork, covered, for another hour or so. Check the meat with a thermometer; when you hit 150° F, baby you're done. No basting, no messing around. Very simple and an easy dish if you need to go do something else, like set the table and give yourself a quick pedicure, before your guests arrive. You will still have time to make the Chunky Apple Fig Chutney (recipe below). It's divine with the pork and highly recommended.

Chunky Apple Fig Chutney

1 large apple, or two medium apples; peeled, cored and chopped into chunks

8 dried figs, any type, snipped into bites

¼ cup agave nectar

¾ cup brown sugar, or turbinado sugar

1 teaspoon cinnamon

Pinch coarse salt

Put all ingredients into a small saucepan and heat through, stirring. Sprinkle in some love while you are at it. Serve alongside the pork or by the spoonful for breakfast on toast if you are in a rush and out of jam.

My Perfect Pairing: Frick Syrah

From my notes: *Peonies, sweetness, cherry, bicycle tire, bubblegum powder, gingerbread cookies and maple syrup*

Inspiration From My Notes: Powerless

And now I sit in my home with candles lit. No power from the strong, crazy push of wind that ran through the world this morning. Lord knows how long it will be out. Don't much care; I'm enjoying keeping up with things in the silence of powerlessness.

The fire licks in front of me and the dog is curled up on my legs, stretched out toward it. The rocks in my Manhattan shift and slip like little icebergs sweating up the glass … and where does my mind wander? Of course. To him.

I'm so with him. The relationship is effortless—we can stay up all night together making love or sitting in a hot tub or watching eclipses—then sleep a bit and get up together and do it all again at the same level, same pace, same intensity. We go from wild and breaking furniture to him rocking me gently and stroking my hair with his strong builder's hands—he is the most tender man on the planet—he's my match, he's my mate. I have known it this whole time. He's the one who can run with me, and see it all and do it all and be it all—and be nothing, and be in the middle of nothing and yet have everything. We have shared some of the most moving moments of my life. And we are only getting started.

I hope it rains all night. If the lights never come back, I think it will be just fine.

Unplug and see what comes up.

Everyday Indulgence: Chicken Cacciatore With Polenta

There are a few recipes in my circle that are held with religious respect, and this is one of them. It is a simple thing, Chicken Cacciatore, a simple, heavenly thing. We like to make it on those evenings when shadows come early and curl up at the windowsills, leaving us inside to dance around the warm kitchen while the flavors of this dish marry each other in a sensual fragrant ceremony.

Ingredients

Whole organic chicken, cut into legs, thighs, wings, breasts, back

Flour, for dredging

Coarse salt and fresh pepper

1 clove garlic, pressed

1 small onion, chopped

2 green peppers, seeded and chopped

2 cups button mushrooms or creminis

1 handful each of fresh rosemary, oregano, thyme

1 cup dry white wine

1 whole tomato, peeled, seeded and chopped

4 tablespoons tomato paste

Polenta

1 cup dry polenta

1 cup water

Coarse salt

Fresh parsley

Prepare the chicken pieces for browning by coating them with salt and pepper and dredging them in flour. Cover the bottom of a large sauté pan with olive oil. Add the pressed garlic and a bit of salt, and bring the oil to medium heat (almost smoking). Brown all sides of each piece of chicken, without cooking through, and set aside. This is a great task to do while trying a new white wine, as you are stuck at the stove for a bit but you may as well have fun. Once all the chicken is browned and set aside, add to the pan the rest of the ingredients except the wine, chopped tomato and tomato paste, and cook for a bit over medium heat. Brown the mushrooms, onions and green pepper nicely, then add the wine and chopped whole tomato. A good rule is that when adding wine to any recipe, take deep inhales of the wine itself and of the pot you are cooking—if they smell good together you can bet the flavors will marry successfully.

Add the tomato paste, and mix everything over medium high heat, as you want the sauce just under a boil at this point so that everything breaks down well. Once the sauce is integrated, add the chicken back into the pan, cover, and simmer until the chicken is tender—about an hour—checking from time to time and adding a little water if needed. Your goal is a nice, thick sauce. Adjust the salt to your liking as you go.

Meanwhile, you have time to make the polenta, which is as easy as rolling off a log, as long as you do not lean over the pot. Simply, bring 1 cup of salted water to a boil, add in 1 cup of polenta (cornmeal), turn the heat to a very low simmer, and stir a bit. The first time I made polenta I was holding the bag under the light of the stove while I stirred the pot slowly. Finding myself without my glasses, I leaned forward to read the directions, my face just over the pot. As I read the words "watch for spitting" suddenly a perfect bubble of boiling polenta erupted directly onto the flesh of my chin. The pain was intense but I was too busy laughing at myself and the irony of what had just occurred to mind much. Lesson learned.

You have a few options for presentation, which will direct the way you make your polenta. You can cook it so that it is still creamy; simply shut off the heat while it is the consistency of Cream of Wheat. For this presentation, make a lush bed of polenta and nestle the chicken and sauce on top. Or, you can go toward the thicker side, cooking until more moisture is simmered out. Once the polenta is done cooking, pour it into an 8-quart mixing bowl; it will firm up and take the form of the bowl as it cools. You can then slice it into wedges and serve with the chicken and sauce on the side. For either serving style, you have the option of adding ½ cup of grated Parmigiano cheese into the polenta at the end of the cooking process if you want to make it a bit richer. Whichever path you take, end with a generous dusting of freshly chopped parsley and prepare to tuck into heaven for a bit.

My Perfect Pairing: Obermoser Hof Grafenleiten Lagrein Riserva

From my notes: *Rabbit ravioli! Oxtails! Dried figs and peach slices, black cherry and tobacco smoke*

Inspiration From My Notes: The Left Edge Of Canada

What an amazing place Vancouver Island is. What an even more amazing place this inn is. With a wine list among the world's best and a kitchen flush with creativity and food of place, what happens here is truly magical.

After an endless dinner one cool night, I sat out on the deck of my room. It was a full-moon evening at the harbor. I tucked in, and watched the most gorgeous moondance on water that I have ever seen. I was out there, wrapped in blankets, alone, when I heard what I thought was a woman singing. She sang a beautiful song, then stopped. Then started again. It was haunting and amazing. I thought perhaps it was a very spiritual woman simply moved to song— perhaps on full moons, celebrating the cycles. Whatever the reason, I enjoyed the concert. The sounds picked up and dropped down without order, yet with perfect timing, like the glittering diamonds on water that the moonbeams made below me. The closer I listened, in fact, yes, that song did move just in time to the gently undulating surface of the water. I finally got cold through my bones and surrendered, crawling into bed between my warm lover and our tiny, toasty dog.

The next day at breakfast, the innkeeper raised his eyebrows as I mentioned the weird concert. He told me he that he had heard that song once, 20 years ago. He said that only a few people have heard it at all. They happened to all have in common sleeping in that corner room and, in his opinion, perhaps a level of awareness lost on some others. He said, "You heard the Sirens," and added quite matter-of-factly, "I'm not surprised."

If you only prepare yourself for what you expect to happen, only the expected will happen. Allow your senses to open, and see who or what shows up. You may want to change the sheets now.

Everyday Indulgence: Foraged Wild West Coast Mussels Steamed in Riesling and Coriander Broth

This delicious recipe is a gracious contribution from my wise friend Sinclair P. at the Sooke Harbour House on Wiffen Spit Beach in British Columbia.

Ingredients

1.5 pounds open surf mussels, scrubbed and cleaned, beards removed (substitute any other mussel)

2 tablespoons sunflower seed oil, organic, cold-pressed

1 clove garlic, peeled, sliced paper-thin

½ cup assorted chiles, stems and seeds removed, julienned [50% hot chiles such as (cayenne (red), jalapeño (green), Hungarian wax (white); 50% mild chiles such as bullhorns (yellow), bell (orange), shepherd (red)]

3 tablespoons Vietnamese coriander

3 tablespoons spearmint leaves

Riesling Broth

Total volume needed is 1 ½ cups

Riesling, (1) 750-ml bottle, dry to off-dry

1 ½ cups clear fish stock

1 ½ cups water

3 tablespoons Brandy or Cognac

4 stalks lemon grass (East Indian)

8 stalks Vietnamese coriander, with leaves

8 stalks spearmint, with leaves

1 tablespoon coriander seeds, fresh or dried

1 tablespoon dried fennel seeds, or 3 tablespoons fresh fennel seeds

1 teaspoon chile flakes

1 head garlic, peeled and crushed

1 medium onion, skin removed, roughly chopped

1 medium carrot, peeled and roughly chopped

1 tablespoon buckwheat honey

Let Diana Krall set the sexy, moody tone for this dish and its preparation. To make the broth, place all the ingredients for it in a heavy-bottomed pot and bring to a boil over high heat. Keep an eye if you end up slow-dancing in the kitchen, and when it reaches boiling point, reduce to a simmer and cook for about 30 minutes, during which time you can continue dancing. Then, strain through a fine mesh strainer into another pot, place the pot over high heat, and reduce by half. Again, dancing optional.

To steam the mussels, place them in a large, heavy-bottomed pot with a lid over high heat. Add the sunflower seed oil, and heat to the smoking point. Add the garlic and chiles, and stir vigorously until the ingredients are slightly charred. This will take approximately 30 seconds, so I recommend taking a break from dancing in order to focus. If someone wants to stand behind you with their hands clasped lightly around your waist, that would be all right. Have them help you toss the mussels. On top of this goes the Riesling broth. Cover immediately, and reduce to medium heat.

Cook until all the mussels open, approximately 4 minutes. The mussels will give up a liquor, a sweet briny nectar, increasing your broth, which then must be reduced to about 1 ½ cups. Once all of the mussels have opened, reduce the broth, lid removed, for about 1 minute.

Add the coriander and spearmint to the pot, and toss until wilted; this should take 10 to 15 seconds. Serve immediately. Feeding the mussels to each other from the pot you cooked them in right at the stove is totally acceptable, but another option would be to mound them in a big bowl, tuck a baguette under your arm and head to sit in front of a roaring fire with a bottle of wine, thanking Ms. Krall as you leave the kitchen.

My Perfect Pairing: Venturi Schultz Chicks & Hens Brut Natural

From my notes: *Creamsicle! And clean, clear mineral, like sucking on a little stone from beside the ocean, just as soothing as her shore song*

ADVENTURES ARE DECADENT

I like to keep a little bag packed at all times. Nothing fancy, just a case holding the essentials to cover a few days. My theory and practice is that if you are prepared to travel at any given moment, then each moment suddenly becomes an invitation for adventure. While I love a rowdy escapade away from home, I also find you don't always need to travel far. Sometimes, the best adventures can be just moments away. It's your own willingness to open up to the scene around you that counts. Enjoy the journey of a brand new path, even when it may at first seem the same one you've taken a thousand times before.

Inspiration From My Notes: One Italian Courtyard

I lived a decadent life for a time in the green hills of Italy. My student-based family there was a mess made of some savage and evangelistic poets, a few scholars wound tight and ready to burst, a pack of philosophers passionate about everything from coffee pots to bombs, and two musicians tough from payless jobs washing wine bottles with nothing but sand and icy water in a magic and rugged place deep in the hills of Umbertide. That kind of life left your hands chapped and hard, but the view was worth the pain. Here are a few notes from those days.

It's late in the night of the 10th of Febrario; just back from a party at M's house. Last week I met his upstairs neighbor and I am in total lust, and he was there again tonight. He studies chemistry and I found out why, his is excellent. We talked for hours and drank wine together in the narrow hallway, til he finalmente (finally) said, "I know a place; follow me." We went into the kitchen and climbed out of a high, high window (so high we had to stand on a chair to reach it and then pull up and out to clear the sill) and into the courtyard we dropped. At the time I thought nothing of it, but now I am wondering—isn't there a door somewhere to make it easier to get out there? Anyway, we were out of the house, the loud crowd shrieking and laughing and singing behind the wall behind us. It was cool outside, but we were quite hot. There was a small patch of grass, a table and a few delicate, bare-branched trees against the billowing gray sky. I sat on the edge of that table with him between my legs and learned all about kissing Italian boys. Fierce. He's seven years younger than me. I asked him if he knew that. He said he did not care. And actually, I don't think he did.

Let decadence find you in unexpected places. If you have to stand on a chair and climb out of a window to get there, you may want to grab a bottle of wine on your way out.

Everyday Indulgence: Spaghetti With Garlic, Olive Oil

The best thing about this dish is you can be a little drunk from wine or making love, or both, and throw it together without much trouble.

Ingredients

4 cloves garlic, minced fine or pressed	Big handfuls of spaghetti, depending on the size of your crowd
Olive oil	
Coarse salt and fresh pepper	Fresh basil if it is summer; if not, omit

Try not to giggle too loudly when you come in the door of your flat, so that you do not wake your sleeping roommates, unless you want their company. If you do, introduce your entry with a loud round of Ciao! Siamo tornati! and then promptly knock something over in the hallway. Once you are safely in the land where all goodness comes from (also known as la cucina, the kitchen), hunt in the cupboards for that good bottle you know your roommate has stashed somewhere (preferably before he or she stumbles out of his or her room to join your rowdy party). Why is it that we always break into someone else's good bottle when we have already that evening had several other bottles of our own that we thought were good? It is a mystery even to me.

Keep looking while someone fills a large pot with water, salts it and gets it going. Once the wine is served and the lid is on, it's a waiting game filled with the small task of mincing a little garlic and chopping up a little basil, taking care with the knife if you sharpened it recently. In fact, use the dull one tonight. The pasta goes into the big boil, and you hope the good wine holds out a little longer (it never does). Meanwhile, give a generous donation of olive oil to a sauté pan, and add the garlic. Over medium heat, lightly brown the garlic with some salt. When the pasta is al dente, drain it, and add it back in the pot—among stories of the disco, who was with who and who was not there—then do a big tossing with the garlic and oil, and more if needed to lubricate everything generously. Incorporate a few absentminded flicks of salt and a couple twists of pepper while you add to the stories over your shoulder.

Now you are sitting on mismatched kitchen chairs in low light at the big round table—too big for the room—a perpetual magnet for eccentrics and full of them now. Bread has been produced from somewhere, and everyone is laughing, smoking hand-rolled cigarettes and telling stories. The good stuff is gone, but no one cares as they eat plates of garlic pasta as though back from the work of plowing fields by hand and are drinking now from the big common jug of wine that is always there on this table, in the center of it all. This wine, which has always been just good, suddenly tastes absolutely fabulous in the rowdy glow of this impromptu middle-of-the-night-party, which shows no signs of slowing as the jug is still half full.

My Perfect Pairing: Giovanni Allegrini Recioto della Valpolicella Classico

From my notes: *Sausage pizza! Fresh dough, fennel, tomatoes, sweet onions, all! Blackberries, black cherry, plum and prune explode on the palate*

Inspiration From My Notes: A Wine Country Bike Ride

Today we ended up on our bikes all day! We hopped on our cruisers this morning, planning to just take a ride around the vineyard. I had work I "needed" to go back and do, but suddenly we went right out of the driveway and before I knew it we were across the street tasting wine just like tourists. (I made sure to spit.) It was so much fun! I wore only my sundress and flip-flops and I had nothing with me but a lip gloss tucked in my bra strap. It was so deliciously simple. Warmed up by the first stop, we came back to the winery ready for more adventure. We took the trail behind the vineyard to a side street, popping out like 10-year-olds onto a back road. We cruised all over, visiting tasting rooms and crunching along Calistoga's gravelly back roads. I loved it! We were kids again, free, simple. Why hadn't we done this sooner? Too busy working all the time. When we arrived back, just before the tasting room closed, we met another couple that had stopped in for one last taste of Sauvignon Blanc before heading to their hotel. Inspired by our decadent day, and hungry from the ride, we decided on the spot to pop some bubbles and share a bite. I ran upstairs and put together a voluptuous charcuterie platter mounded with cured meats and strongly scented chunks of cheese. In 10 minutes we were all best friends and toasting to our collective good health. Wine is a wonderful connector. The Palisades glowed their purple magenta at us and we just sat and smiled, yes, we smiled a lot.

For me, only one thing compares to the wild freedom I feel on the back of a horse: cruising around on a bicycle! Do yourself a favor and get out on your bike! You don't have to go crazy and start commuting to your office daily in the pitch dark like my sister does (bless her fit heart), just pull it out and ride around the block once. Put a basket on the front or the back and use it to get groceries. Ride it to coffee with your girlfriends. Ride it to the park to meet your new bf. Bonus: Your cheeks will be rosy and your eyes will sparkle with sheer delight when you hop off that seat and he will love your natural good looks. My, how wholesome you are!

Everyday Indulgence: Ultimate Anytime Cheese Plate

The trick to the perfect cheese plate is to always be prepared to make one. Don't wait for an invitation to try those locker-room scented globs of oozy cheese you've been eyeing sideways at the market. A good rule is to always keep three to four different styles of cheese in your fridge. Aged cheese is great as it lasts a very long time. But so does a delicate chèvre if left unopened.

Make This: The Best Cheese Plate Ever

We entertain a lot in Napa Valley. When you live above a public space, especially a tasting room, it's like having an open invitation to a party that can begin at any given moment taped to your front door. (For this reason, I work out early in the morning, so it's over with and I can get on with anything that arrives.) And we love cheese. I mean, we love it. Why? Because you can whip up a killer cheese plate any time, and it looks and tastes amazing. We are lucky in Napa to have very good cheese selections at hand, so we regularly stock up at our local markets and cheese shops. Cheese is easy to serve with wine if you stick to a few rules. The main one: Keep the weight of the wine equal to the strength of the cheese.

You don't need that many cheeses to put a great cheese plate together. Remember that all cheeses fall into just a few categories: aged & hard; stinky & soft; creamy & soft; mild or rich & neither hard nor soft but somewhere in the middle.

Here are some cheeses we almost always have on hand.
Aged & Hard: Beemster, Parmigiano, aged Gouda (love this), Asiago
Stinky & Soft: Morbier, Point Reyes Blue
Creamy & Soft: Goat cheeses by Cypress Grove
Mild & in the Middle: Dubliner!
Rich & in the Middle: Aged goat cheeses by Cypress Grove

To make a killer cheese plate, simply select a few of the cheeses from the list above. To make it interesting, make sure you have at least one cheese from at least three of the four categories. Add the following items to your cheese plate in any combination or quantity and you're done! Enjoy the party!

Cured olives; green picolinas, deep dark kalamatas, cured big fat green ones
Dried and cured meats, mustard

Almonds, filberts, pecans or pistachios

Dried fruits such as dates, prunes, Turkish apricots, bing or Rainier cherries

Honey! Experiment with them to find a style you like—there are so many available: clover, wildflower, orange …

Pickles: Gherkins are a must, sweet midgets are fun, too. I have even served capers alongside cheese for a salty slant if I'm out of pickles.

Compote or fruit spread is great too if you do not have honey or just want something sweet and different.

Simply plate all this on a pretty platter and serve with whatever crackers you have. I like big rounds of cracker bread as it never goes stale and is full of whole grains. I break mine in rustic hunks and put them in a bowl in a stack, upright, like a crazy deck of cards. Voilà! Now go and relax with your friends.

My Perfect Pairing: Envy Wines Calistoga Estate Petite Sirah

From my notes: *Honey, treacle nose, bad boy cookies with raspberry jam, tons of earth and very foresty at the same time, love! Salmon fat, Buster's at noon in Calistoga, cherry Coke!*

Inspiration From My Notes: Berry Picking

I rode out of the yard about six that evening on Dawn, my buckskin pony. She was nearly a horse, but an inch kept her from claiming the title, and I believe that was the root of all her sourness for the rest of her almost-horse life. All that rage simmered just below the surface of her smooth honey-colored hide, which ended in every direction on her body in glistening jet black. I loved her insanely. She knew every trail within a two-hour ride of my house, which was about as far as I was allowed to go at age 14. Lucky for me, my latest crush lived within these riding limits.

But tonight I didn't have boys on my mind. I was going to pick blackberries. I had two empty sacks hanging from my saddlehorn and I knew just the spot that was going to fatten them both up. We wound our way against the treeline in the endless farm fields that lie just across the street from our house. Along the cool edge of the woods we slipped, careful not to stomp on anything grown on purpose. In less than 30 minutes we were there. It was the thickest patch of blackberries I had ever seen. They hung heavy, pulling the dense, prickered vines over from their weight. My only competition was the birds around me, and even they couldn't eat enough of the bounty to make a difference.

I nosed Dawn into the thicket, tied the reins in a knot, and right from my perch in the saddle started picking. It was easy work. She munched grass while I filled the sacks as full as I could, moving her when I needed to with little more than a knee nudge. I knew the berries on the bottoms of the sacks would be smashed, but that's a risk you take when you have such abundance on your hands. I ate as I picked, of course. They were hard to resist, fat as bumblebees and sugary. I liked the way the little seeds popped in my mouth in tiny explosions of tanninlike contrast against the sweet. I would remember this moment years later with my nose in a glass of ripe mountain Cabernet from Napa County. When I truly couldn't add more to my sacks, and the sun had shifted low, I pushed the ponyhorse toward home with my mind. That was all she needed. She knew the way. I closed my eyes and let her take me, following the rhythm of her black-rimmed ears as dark as my berry-stained hands.

There is something very rewarding and relaxing about harvesting your own food. You naturally fall into the rhythm of the seasons, and the connection can have a very meditative effect. The taste of a strawberry plucked and still warm from the sun that worked to make it plump is a singular sensation worth experiencing. Take your senses to the spa with a trip to a local berry farm or even a pick-your-own produce lot. Perhaps you can step outside and see what your own garden has given you. A farmer's market is the next best thing, if you don't have enough time to go and pick.

Everyday Indulgence: Blackberry Crisp

These days when the blackberries come in near my horses' pasture, I usually pick every day. They are so thick, and I swear, the more I pick the more there are the next day. What a problem to have! This is a simple recipe that will help keep a blackberry abundance in check. You can also toss blackberries into your morning pancakes, enrich basic, creamy yogurt, or concoct exotic cocktails with muddled berries and all kinds of goodies (look up the Southern Gentleman recipe from the Sazarac Bar in the Roosevelt Hotel in New Orleans).

Ingredients

6 cups fresh blackberries (substitute any type of berry, or even sliced peaches or apples)

3 tablespoons turbinado sugar or brown sugar

1 ½ tablespoons vanilla extract

½ teaspoon cinnamon

⅓ cup whole wheat flour or spelt flour

Topping

4 tablespoons turbinado or brown sugar

1 teaspoon cinnamon

½ teaspoon nutmeg

½ teaspoon salt

6 tablespoons cold butter

1 cup rolled oats

⅓ cup flour

½ cup chopped walnuts

When your sister comes to town, whip up this dessert; it's easy, healthy and you can spend quality time with her in the kitchen. Preheat the oven to 400° F and fix a pot of coffee. Mix up the berries, sugar, cinnamon, vanilla and flour. Pour into an ovenproof dish, any variety. You can split the recipe up into individual crisps if you prefer. Bake the fruit for 35 minutes or so until it bubbles. While you make the topping, have a cup of coffee and talk with your sister about your mom or the other sisters who are not there. Mix the flour, sugar, spices and salt in a bowl. Cut the butter into the mixture with a pastry blender until it starts to crumble, then add the oats and most of the nuts, mixing with your hands if you need to so that the topping forms small chunks. You can chill the topping off at this point for a bit in the fridge if you are still waiting for the berries to bubble. When the fruit is ready, remove, top with the oat-nut mixture, and pop back it into the oven for another

10 to 15 minutes, until it goes golden and crunchy on top. Since you have a theme going, you have an excuse to serve your sister the famous New Orleans Southern Gentlemen, a cocktail that includes muddled blackberries and a lot of whiskey. Make a small pitcher on ice to smooth out the edges, and plate up the crisp. Move the party outside and finish your stories under the jasmine blossoms. Only the two of you would do something like this.

My Perfect Pairing: Château Lafite Rothschild Pauillac

From my notes: *Right from bubbles to Lafite ... perfect fall leaves and ... oh, subtle and lush, elegance and power in one, restrained power, yes! Like Isabella in harness. Really lovely this*

Inspiration From My Notes: Many Ways To Worship In Italy

A story pulled from my Italian flat days.

Went to the disco tonight. After dinner here at the house (as always loud and crazy messes and too many cigarettes), we put six in a car that held only four. I was the smallest and had to ride lying on top of the other three people in the back seat, my belly to the roof. With my neck twisted and my head pressed close to the back window, I watched the shadowy Italian countryside slip by in the night. It was scary, and I will probably leave this part out when I tell Mom. We got there and it was insane. Discos in Italy are quite surreal, and the people were all so beautiful, or maybe I was just overwhelmed with the lights. We stayed late, then it was back toward home for breakfast, which had nothing to do with pancakes at Denny's. We went to a café and had black espressos, tiny little rums and cappuccinos and pastries, all while standing straight up! The boys bought bottles of cold Champagne and we piled back into the car. All through the streets of Perugia we drove, streets narrow (too narrow for us!) and twisted. Though I know the city, I was totally lost. We made our way to a gorgeous place, a temple—was it really the temple of the Clitunno? Did we go that far? No, we could not have …, could we? But—it was a temple in moonlight and it was getting near dawn. I remember the steps and the water nearby and the grass, too. An expanse of grass to my left, yes I see it. And drinking Champagne right from the bottle and making out with that elegant man, never forgetting him with his long coattails spread wide behind him as he spun in the night, dancing in the glow, spinning in the dark, the lights of the city all around us like diamonds sparkling, worshiping together in our own way.

If in Italy, someone asks if you want to go to breakfast, they rarely mean pancakes and coffee and it often begins the evening before. Adventures are decadent. What was your last one like?

Everyday Indulgence: Almond Biscotti

I learned to make biscotti during my decadent days at 239 East King Street. I learned to dip them in deep red wine while living in Italy years later (thanks Giampiero). This is a recipe from my good friend Debbie.

Ingredients

3 cups flour	3 eggs
½ teaspoon baking soda	½ cup sunflower oil
¼ teaspoon salt	1 teaspoon vanilla
1 cup sugar	2 tablespoons aniseed
3 teaspoons baking powder	1 cup chopped almonds

This is a good Saturday morning ritual. Have a cup of coffee on the front steps and make your daily to-do list; since it's Saturday the only rule is to include some work on a personal pleasure goal (interpret that however you desire). Pay attention to the color of the sky, the new shoots arriving in your flowerbed if it's spring, or the lush brush of color there if it's fall, and the sounds of your world (birds? busses? both?). Add to your list "make biscotti," so you have the satisfaction of crossing it off later.

Preheat the oven to 350° F, and open the windows for a little fresh air. Sift together the flour, baking soda and salt and add to it the rest of the dry ingredients. In a separate bowl, mix the eggs, oil and vanilla. Make a dent in the middle of the dry ingredients and add in the egg mixture, stirring well but not overmixing.

With floured hands, form the dough into a rough ball and transfer to a floured surface. Still using your hands, create a flattened log shape about 6 to 7 inches wide and 1-inch tall. Place the log on an ungreased cookie sheet, and bake for about 25 minutes.

Put on some Aretha Franklin and do some housework, or get the guts up to ask out that cute guy you have a crush on, while it bakes. How sexy would it be to invite him over for a bottle of deep red wine and some Italian biscotti you just whipped up? If the conversation heats up, don't forget your oven. You want the cookie to set, but you do not want it hard. It should be a beautiful golden brown when it comes out. Tell him you will call him back.

Remove the log from the oven, and place it on a cutting board. With a sharp serrated knife, carefully cut the log into ¾-inch slices, and flip them onto their sides. Back into the oven for 10 minutes more. You may want to spiff up the kitchen now since you now have a date for tonight at your house. Remove the biscotti from the oven, flip again, and bake another 10 minutes. Repeat once more.

Cool the biscotti on a wire rack. They will keep for a very long time in a covered jar and, just like wine, seem to get better with age. Now, look at you! Your kitchen is clean, your home smells amazing, you have a date for tonight and you have completed your to-do list. Good work. You deserve a bike ride. Go outside and play.

My Perfect Pairing: Uccelliera Brunello di Montalcino

From my notes: *Like a 4-H Camp Whitewood bunk bed, earthy but innocent! Dried fruit and leather boots, maybe dry leather boots, really good*

DECADENT SIMPLICITY

Ah the decadence of simplicity. From simple sea salt on warm tomatoes to salty seawater on warm naked shoulders, I have always been a firm believer in "less is more." With your existence stripped bare of all but the essentials you are in the perfect place to tune in. Simplicity results in a calm focus where you can find the sumptuous touch of sleek horsehide in your palm, the crisp taste of sweet ripe apples, the clear sound of a cold night empty save a dazzling meteor shower and your own excited breath.

Inspiration From My Notes: The Darker The Night, The Brighter The Shooting Stars

I lived for a time in Oakville, which except for the famous Oakville grocery and the post office is little more than a crossroads, just about in the middle of Napa Valley. Oakville is really two things: Cabernet, Sauvignon. Enough said. You are completely surrounded by famous and fabulous vineyards. While living there I ran for my health in the vineyards every day, watching the vintage emerge, push, pull and yield. In heat of day or the cool of evening's hushed hues, the scene is simply stunning.

During harvest, the Oakville air heavy with the perfume of fresh crush; I planned an adventure with my love to watch a meteor shower from a cozy spot among the vines. We got up at 3 a.m., bundled up, and hiked with sleeping bags and low-slung chairs into the vineyard across the street to watch the show. And what a show it was! One after another, sometimes two, three, four at once, the shooting stars swept across the deep dark sky. We zipped our bags together and snuggled away the cold night, mesmerized by the dazzle above.

Remember the first time you saw a shooting star? Whose hand were you holding? It is perfectly OK if it was two in the afternoon and in broad daylight. Shooting stars come in all shapes and sizes.

Everyday Indulgence: Chops And Sliced Apples

This is a fabulous recipe for an evening in when it's chilly out. Light some candles, dim the lamps and pretend you are miles from civilization but happen to have a fully functioning kitchen. Lucky you.

Ingredients

2 bone-in pork chops

1 clove garlic, pressed

Coarse salt and fresh pepper

Butter

Calvados

Sugar

Two apples, sliced, and tossed with a squeeze of lemon or lime juice

Lemon or lime juice

This dish is so easy to prepare, you may forget you're cooking, so please don't lean on the stove and catch your apron on fire. Put on some Billie Holiday and make yourself a Manhattan, up. Melt a hunk of butter (at least a few tablespoons) in a skillet. Rub the bone of the chops with the pressed garlic, and salt and pepper the meat. Once the butter is smoky (and just starting to bubble), add the seasoned chops. You're doing this for three reasons: 1.) To sear the meat. 2.) So you have a pan to deglaze. 3.) To make the house smell divine.

Preheat the broiler. Once the meat is seared on both sides, move it to the broiler.

For the sauce, deglaze the pan with a good splash (about ¼ cup) of Calvados, apple brandy or just plain brandy. If you don't have any of the above, toss in what's left of your Manhattan (you may need to add a little more Bourbon if you had it half gone).

In a separate pan, heat more butter and add sugar, apples, cracked pepper and lemon juice (for a touch of acid), and cook this down a little, til the apples soften. Don't forget your broiling chops. Turn them once after 7 to 9 minutes. Warm the sauce back up and add in a little butter to get the right consistency, which should be something like warm caramel on the thin side. Plate the dish with the apples snuggled against the side of the chop, and top the meat with the sauce. Now that your Manhattan is gone, I suggest you pull out that Pinot you have been holding onto and head to the dining room.

My Perfect Pairing: Cave de Rivesaltes Vin Doux 1929

From my notes: *Wow. Hot caramel, corn, peat, dates, honey almond fruitcake, brandied plums, sweet raisin, oranges, Golden Grahams*

Inspiration From My Notes: Learning A New Language Takes Practice

Oh my mother Mary comfort me … Italian man is in the forest … Where is Smokey the Bear when you really need him? There was a party on Friday night and it was assolutamente grande e bella, absolutely great and beautiful. Ho incontrato un ragazzo Italiano, I met a young Italian. Lui e un uomo bravo. He is a good man. E possibile penso ti amo? Can I love you? Mama mia. Aiuta me. Help me.

He is a photographer. We met at a party. I had to take a bus. It took a long time to get there, especially including stopping for paella at friend's, which was excellent. And then the festa, party. The apartment was stuffed full of people and bottles of good red wine and to eat there was only Nutella and crunchy loaves of good bread. It was really perfect.

All night long I spoke Italian. It was literally today, on my way to class, that the language just finally clicked. After these months of living here and going to class, and hearing and speaking in fragments, suddenly it all came together and into clear and sharp focus, certainly preparing me for this exact moment.

I was able to converse smoothly (for the most part) all night. From group to group I chatted, and as I made my way around the room I noticed this very hot man wearing glasses. Artsy. Angular. Sexy. Very late in the night we were standing with our backs to each other, almost touching but facing away, both talking to other people. But with the help of some star alignments, we turned around at the exact same moment, right into each other. Our eyes met. He said only "ciao," long and low. And that was it. After talking forever, he offered to give me a ride home on his Vespa. I have named her Silver. I am in so much trouble.

When you work at something and do not feel like you are making progress quickly enough, have faith. Things usually come together right when you really need them—so enjoy the decadence of the journey. Who knows what's waiting for you?

Everyday Indulgence: Nutella

If you have never tasted the hazelnut chocolaty experience that is Nutella, please, I beg you, go to the store NOW and get some. It may be the most decadent thing to ever happen to toast. That is all I can say here.

My Perfect Pairing: Antinori Toscana Tignanello

From my notes: *Nose is gorgeous flowers, roses, orange water. Dense and tannic, shakes you from your core then gently sets you down; finish rolls out with dusty fruit and murmurs of heat and heavy petting*

Inspiration From My Notes: The Beatles In San Marco Square

We are in Venice. I am attempting to become invisible as I cannot stand the tourist scene and want no part of it. We have spent our days in art museums and in cafés reading and painting and disappearing against the stone walls of the city. Only at night we come alive. Guiseppe is of course making photos. All black and white. We have come for the full moon, which happens tonight. I will write more later.

And now it's later, back in our room, in bed, under thin blankets. G is smoking and drinking wine from a small clear glass. In the dim light I watch the smoke curl. What a night we have had. The moon rose big and full and out we went, slipping among the canals black and deep near our feet. The twisted streets and bridges all weaving together like some old metropolitan tapestry drained of color. G stopping often and shooting things, crouching on his muscular haunches, black-rimmed glasses peeking out of the upturned collar of his coat. And me wide-eyed and taking it all in moment by magical moment. After some time we came upon the expanse of San Marco Square. Even wider than normal in its middle-of-the-night emptiness save a few private couples walking as one and a group of six or so people sitting on the ground in the center of the piazza. Moonlight flooded the scene. There was a man in the center of this group, sitting with legs crossed, a guitar in his hands. And in the stillness of the Venetian moon-drenched night I heard, of all things, the opening notes of Blackbird by the Beatles. Clear, open, unmistakable. "Da, da, da, dadaddada ... *blackbird singing in the dead of night ... take these broken wings and learn to fly* ... ." The acoustics were amazing. It was all I could do to lower myself to the ground, stretch out on my back in my warm woolen coat and listen. "... *all my life, I was only waiting for this moment to arrive* ... ." Guiseppe was at my side. We held hands tightly and gazed up at the moon. Bellisimo. Tomorrow, Trieste.

Tune in.

My Perfect Pairing: Capitel Croce Veneto Anselmi

From my notes: *Light peaches, honeysuckle, melon and mint, vanilla Creamsicle*

Inspiration From My Notes: Sailing On The Zuiderzee

Just returned home from a nice bike ride with Hélène. We went to Durgerdam, Marken and a few other small towns along the way. Today it was so clear what I love! I was so happy as we went along the sea dike. The road follows right alongside the Zuiderzee, and the bike path is on top of the dike. So all around you see water, meadows, cows, sheep and, of course, ponies! I can't express how much I love it all! It feels so right there, amid nature. The sound of the wind singing in the long thin grass. It is just a perfect place to be, sailing along on a bicycle. It is the only thing that comes close to my feelings when up on a horse in an open field, the sun shining down and the breezes all around, and it has its own windsong, a horseback ride does. It is home for me, this feeling. And I am suddenly aware and surprised how much this trip to Amsterdam has helped me in knowing who I am and what it is that moves me. Alone is good. I'm learning far more on this journey than I ever thought I would. More later, tea now.

Getting back to basics is a good way to reconnect with the depth of yourself. In quiet communion with simple gifts around you each day, acknowledge the basis of you. Let your own essence tap in to a place of solid ground and you will soar above the highest clouds.

What are you working on? Are you aware of the journey? Is it already filling you up? Let go of the end, it is far off. Sit up, look around and enjoy the view from the middle.

Everyday Indulgence: Roosmirijnhof #4 Cheese Fondue From Hélène

An evening of good cheese fondue begins with a day at the Albert Cuyp market located, logically, on the lively Albert Cuypstraat in Amsterdam. My dear friend Hélène, whom I lived with just outside of the city one extraordinary fall and winter of my life, introduced me to the charming chaos of this large open-air street market. Here we bought all kinds of things—raw canvas for my paintings, colorful umbrellas, funky hats, but mostly we hunted for deals of the edible variety. I loved going with her and wandering the stalls, learning the Dutch language like a little girl, reading the vegetables' names aloud with Hélène's guidance on pronunciation: Selderij! Uien! Worteljes! *(Celery! Onion! Little carrots!)* We laughed at my practice and indulged in stroopwafels, made fresh and hot while you watched, your tongue taking on a life of its own with the longing for that hot, sugary treat—a singular flavor worth every calorie involved. This unique and luscious morsel has been dug up in my collective memory of scents and flavors a few times over the years since then while taking wine tasting notes. Delicious. The cheese stalls were our favorite, and the kaas was goed, *the cheese was good.*

Ingredients

2 cups white wine

2 to 3 ounces Emmenthaler and Gruyère cheese per person

1 clove garlic, pressed

½ teaspoon nutmeg

Fresh pepper (and coarse salt, optional)

2 tablespoons Kirsch liqueur

Cornstarch, for thickening

Here is Hélène's recipe in her own words:

Put wine in pan, add cheese, stir until melting, add garlic, nutmeg, pepper and liqueur, thicken with cornstarch. Adding some salt is a question of taste. It becomes a bit sweet because of the Kirsch and it depends on the wine you use. In principle, you can use all kinds of white wine.

Put a French stick in the oven, and when it is nice and crispy, cut it, and dip it in the cheese fondue. You can include sliced green apple and any assortment of crudités for dipping, too. And dat is dat.

My Perfect Pairing: J. Dumangin Fils Champagne Chigny-les-Roses

From my notes: *Smells like a Sazarac but it's Champagne! Creamy, minerally, neutral, fascinating*

Inspiration From My Notes: A Talk With A Flea-Bitten Gray

My horse Bella lives the decadent life. She has a gorgeous pasture surrounded by nothing but trees, blackberry bushes and other horses. She is happy as can be, with lots of room to stretch out and be a horse. I love to go and hang out in Bella's pasture with her at dusk. Sometimes I just go and mosey around the pasture near her, quietly melting into the landscape of swishing tails, soft horse breath and shifting light. One particularly gorgeous night, with a huge full moon low in the sky above the tree line, I stood at the slope of her shoulder with one hand resting on her smooth, speckled gray hide. The only sounds were the birds and the steady "munch, munch" of Bella and her pasture mate as they ate their big pile of hay. Mesmerized by the moon and the quality of the light that night, I could not help but express this to my equine companions. "Pretty moon tonight, huh?" The question slipped out of my mouth and as I realized who I was talking to, Bella surprised and delighted me by swinging her big graceful head up and out of her hay and taking a good look directly at the moon—checking it out for herself while she continued to munch. There was no mistake. Every hair on my body stood up. I had gone to the other side and she had let me in. Delicious.

Stop talking and start communicating. Check in with the rhythm of the wind. Doesn't it sound like your own breath?

My Perfect Pairing: Montirius Gigondas

From my notes: *Warm, wonderful horseskin, vanilla cream soda, and somehow, oddly, the smells of Glen Ellen*

Inspiration From My Notes: At Our Beach House

Just back from sunset. My love and the dog and I climbed the high bluff at my favorite secret beach tonight a half an hour before dusk, with the Pacific wind howling all around us. I questioned my sanity as the gusts tried to bite through my furry parka. In that coat, the one from the secondhand shop, with the real fur–lined hood, I felt like an Eskimo, with our tiny dog pulling me along behind her at the end of the leash. My man had the quilt over both shoulders and carried a basket stuffed with chilled Riesling and cheeses, as we had stopped at the market on the way. We quickly found our spot. I only know this special sheltered place in the dunes from among the hundreds around because I have the view behind it branded into my visual memory, having sketched it for over an hour on a perfectly calm, early fall day. It's funny how you know a thing intimately when you have drawn it.

When we arrived, we unfurled the quilt like a sail, catching and flipping, wrestling it down and jumping on top of it. Finally low enough, and protected on the ocean side by a soft mound of sea grass, we no longer heeded the mighty wind, gusting above us. All that was left was the crashing ocean view. The dog trotted around triumphantly and inspected our new home, until the cheeses came out and distracted her from rabbit tracks and driftwood dens. We huddled together, keeping warm in each other's laughter and eyes, eventually putting the dog inside the protection of the empty picnic basket, her head sticking out comically like a furry jack-in-the-box. The wind was wild, like it should be with all that ocean to glide over by the time it met us. Wild until just before the sun slipped. Then it was still and calm all around. What a lovely end to a lovely day.

Do you remember the last time you watched the day end? You don't have to make a big deal of it, but you can if you want to. Sunset is so powerful— it's one of the only points of the day that you are faced with a physical image of the passing of time, which beckons us to slow down and be right there with it. Can you do it this evening? Where?

Everyday Indulgence: Grilled Salmon On A Bed Of Rosemary

This is my variation of salmon grilled on a cedar plank. I don't have a cedar plank. What I do have is a lot of rosemary.

Ingredients

Wild salmon fillets

Olive oil

Coarse salt and fresh pepper

Lemon

A few big bunches of fresh rosemary*

This is a great dish to make when you trim back your garden!

Open your window a crack. Rinse the salmon, and prepare a little brine deep enough to cover the fish. Lay the meat in the saltwater, and go sit outside for a while. Have a glass of Chenin Blanc and enjoy the evening while brining your fish. Light the grill, and remember to grab about three big handfuls of rosemary on your way inside. (If desired, make a nice, simple salad, cover it, and stick it in the fridge.)

Create a flat pan out of aluminum foil, the size of your fish. Remove the fish from the brine, coat it with olive oil and salt and pepper to taste, and center it to rest in the foil pan. Create a bed of rosemary directly on the grill. Place the salmon in its foil pan atop the bed, and surround the fish with a wreath of rosemary inside the pan as well. Keep the flame low, so that the rosemary does not catch on fire immediately. What you want is some light smoking, so a little smolder is OK.

Close the lid of the grill, and sip your wine. Your raised kitchen window should allow just enough of the rosemary smoke to perfume your home with its delicious scent. The fish should be done in about 10 minutes. I like it medium-rare, which is moist and delicious; overcook it, and you will have tough, dry, salmon jerky (which you may want for a road trip but not for dinner). Remove the salmon from the grill and let it rest for a bit. If the weather allows, eat outside to enjoy the perfumed smoke from the grill and the last light of day. If the weather is cool, go in and you just may think you are outside, since you had the good sense to let in a little of that smoky nose while you cooked.

My Perfect Pairing: Stage Left The Go Getter

From my notes: *White Rhône-style blend, peaches, apricots, intense honeysuckle palate, a Fourth of July picnic soul and a petticoat heart— delicious! I question its temperature: room. Question is, which room?*

DECADENCE OF THE SEASONS

There is something to be said for the unique decadence which one can find in any season. From the muddy perfume of spring, teasing us to take advantage of the fertile atmosphere, to the luscious heat of summer, ripening our crops and keeping clothing to a minimum, the decadence surrounds. On it carries as fall wants fires and meats for braising while we nuzzle near the hearth and talk of harvest. The hush of winter may be my favorite decadence of all, finally sinking into the peace of warm ovens and dark days where dreams are built in the glow of candlelight, preparing for the next cycle once again. And on it goes always this way.

Inspiration: Spaghetti Straps And Iced Mint Tea

Growing up in the Midwest, nothing inspired me more than the long hot days of summer. I absolutely loved everything about the season, from dewy morning horseback rides to warm evenings that lingered endlessly, a gift of extra time from nature. When I ventured to the West Coast for good, I settled in Northern California, next to the sea, not realizing what kind of sacrifice she was going to ask of me. While I would never give up my home here, her new weather rhythms took some getting used to. On my first Christmas Eve there, my neighbor cheerfully mowed his lawn. The incongruence of the smell of freshly cut grass while I was busy wrapping gifts was a shock. I snapped the windows shut, turned up Burl Ives, and lit some cinnamon candles to cope.

Eventually, I accepted it for the most part. I forgot all about driving in the snow and happily gardened in the rain myself in December. But summer was still a different story. Where my coastal home is, the Pacific sets the temperature at a chilly 50-something in July and August. When it heats up inland, we are wrapped in fog. Fourth of July fireworks? I don't think so. Sunbathing at the beach, why, it's just right there!? Not really. Ever the optimist, I would trick myself into enjoying even the July fog. I turned up Christmas carols all summer and happily made pots of black bean chili in my cozy kitchen, waiting for September so I could sit outside again. There is nothing like the bright fall on the Pacific Coast. Truly stunning.

Just when I could barely remember what a late drive for ice cream felt like, I discovered wine country—and got my summers back. Weekend by weekend I reclaimed the heat, with a vengeance. I vowed not to take blue skies for granted and sat by the pool for days on end, baking under a thick coat of sunscreen. I drank my coffee on the patio in the morning. I dragged my computer outside and worked there in the afternoon. I went to every dinner party I was invited to, lingering in the last heat of the day.

Now I spend half my time in the wine country. I love it. While the change of seasons is not as dramatic as what I grew up with, they happen here. Now I understand why seasons are so important to me; I found that out by losing them for awhile. It's the contrast that makes them all so special.

Celebrate decadence all year. What season are you in? What makes it sing?

Everyday Indulgence: Vita's Fried Chicken

My grandma kept the cooking of hot foods to a minimum in the summer months; it was always just too darn hot! She made one exception on a weekly basis, as regular as clockwork: fried chicken. For that we were eternally grateful. My sister and I were always enlisted to help with the breading of the meat, as there were tasks for everyone who wanted to play a part. One of our favorite jobs was the smashing of the Saltine crackers she used for the breading, which imparted a wonderful saltiness hard to recreate with any other breading ingredient. The golden-fried chickens were her solution to freeing up an afternoon for other things. In the summer, that was usually reading her garden magazines and cookbooks on the back porch. In the fall and winter it was football, as she was raving mad for the sport. She always made everything in the morning and we could all decide later if we wanted our drumsticks hot or cold while she relaxed near the big, humming metal fan that sat by her feet all summer, or cheered her team on with a chicken leg of her own, waving it like a wild pom pom in boisterous support from the living room.

Ingredients

1 whole organic chicken, cut into frying pieces, or chicken parts if you prefer, skin optional

2 whole eggs

¾ cup whole milk (from the Amish family down the street)

Coarse salt and fresh pepper

Paprika

1 cup flour

1 stacked pack of Saltine crackers, crushed to crumbs in a Ziploc bag

Olive oil, for frying

Find your little sister in the yard and let her know her help is needed in the kitchen, and to please wash her hands first. Dial in a good station on the white clock-radio, and pour a cold glass of homemade iced tea for refreshing inspiration. In a bowl large enough for dunking the biggest chicken part you have, whisk together the two eggs, milk, salt and pepper and a generously sprinkle of paprika. On a plate, mix the flour with a little salt and pepper. On another plate, dump the cracker crumbs in a mound, carefully refining the ones that escaped the wrath of the rolling pin during the crushing process.

To bread the chicken, dredge it first in the seasoned flour mixture, and then dip and coat in the egg bath. Once all surfaces have been egged, roll in the cracker crumbs to cover each piece with a decent layer of crunchy goodness.

In a large frying pan, heat your oil (I use a lot of good olive oil for this), which should be a couple of inches deep. As the chicken comes off the breading line, place it in the hot oil over medium heat. Watch the chicken closely; as it turns golden, flip the pieces to cook evenly. I start with the largest pieces first. As your chicken fries to perfection, move the pieces over to a rack for draining; use yesterday's newspaper to catch the extra oil beneath. Try not to eat the wings as they come out of the oil. (Yes, just try.) Salt again if you like, and serve hot now or cold later, with side dishes all proper or you just standing with one hand on the open refrigerator door and the cool air going up your skirt. There are no more rules for fried chicken. Irresistible.

My Perfect Pairing: Curran Grenache Blanc

From my notes: *Honeysuckle, bubble-gum powder, beach house porch, clover nectar, citrus, sea smoke*

Inspiration From My Notes: A Perfect Bowl Of Soup

One of my favorite spots has always been a quaint, lovely bistro located in the much-touted restaurant scene of Yountville, in Napa Valley. Located in the center of the valley, it's a great spot to stop midday and catch a bite before continuing on your wine-tasting adventures.

The dish?

Ah. There is only one tomato soup in the whole world this good.

What a way to spend a harvest season afternoon … in the cozy, cottagey feeling back room, maybe near the fireplace tucked neatly into a corner, sipping Champagne and lounging in a luscious bowl of velvety tomato soup. Yes, it comes with nearly the same amount of fat grams as a pair of glazed doughnuts, but sometimes (when the air starts to turn cool and the sun sets around seven) it's exactly the right thing to do. So do it. Don't stop at the soup. Everything is outrageous.

Decadent dining doesn't usually happen over the sink. Even a grilled cheese will taste better if you use your nice plates, a real linen napkin and good stemware. I recommend adding some Gruyère, prosciutto and thinly sliced tomato to your basic cheddar. Yum.

Everyday Indulgence: (My) Best Tomato Soup
With Cheesy Crostini

Some say that the most decadent comfort-food marriage is the classic grilled cheese and tomato soup. I must agree. This is a good use of the end of summer's tomato crop as you head into fall.

Ingredients

2 pounds ripe tomatoes, coarsely chopped

⅓ cup butter, plus 3 tablespoons, reserved

1 ½ large yellow onions, sliced

5 cloves garlic

2-6 ounce cans tomato paste

½ teaspoon fresh thyme, chopped fine (use more if dried)

¼ teaspoon fresh oregano, chopped fine (use more if dried)

½ cup water

2 tablespoons sugar* (if the tomatoes are not very ripe)

½ cup whole milk

2 cups half-and-half

2 tablespoons Cognac (2 nice splashes from the bottle)

Coarse salt

Ground white pepper

Shredded cheese (Parmigiano, cheddar, Gruyère etc.)

Slices from a French bâtard, 2 per serving

Run like hell from the car to the door to avoid getting drenched in the rain on your way in. Once inside the warm house, shake off the workday and settle into your cozy place for the evening. Ah yes, fall has arrived. It's time for tomato soup. Ready for dinner? Why yes I am.

The whole thing is quite simple. Prepare the onions. Melt ⅓ cup butter in a large stockpot over medium-low heat. Add the onions, cover, and cook for about 5 minutes without browning them. While they cook, chop the tomatoes. When the onions are ready, add the tomatoes, garlic, 1 can of tomato paste, oregano, thyme, and the water (and sugar if your tomatoes are not as ripe as they could be). Simmer over low heat for 30 to 40 minutes, until the tomatoes and onions are very soft. Consider lighting a fire and taking a hot bath now if you are frozen from the newly rainy weather, with a glass of bubbles. Just remember to set the timer. That's better. Ah, don't you feel like one of those little tomatoes in the pot? There's the bell, back to the kitchen.

Shut off the heat, and puree the soup in a blender, a cup at a time, while adding the second can of tomato paste a few tablespoons at a time with each cup in the blender. Strain the batches through a sieve into a clean pot to remove the skins and seeds. Your soup will be so velvety, so smooth! Add the milk, half-and-half, 3 tablespoons butter, cognac, salt and white pepper to taste. Return the soup to a boil then reduce heat to low. Stir from time to time while you make your crostini.

Turn on the broiler, and add another log to the fire. On a baking sheet lined with foil, place rounds of bread with both sides buttered. Salt them just a bit, and place the sheet under the broiler. Watch for browning—it will only take a minute. Flip the bread once, and brown again. Ladle the soup into oven-proof bowls and top each with a generous handful of shredded cheese. Top each slice of bread with cheese as well. Place the bowls on the same sheet as the crostinis and brown everything one more time. Carefully remove the bowls of soup when the tops go crispy and turn the color of honey, and serve with the crostini on the side. Caution! Hot stuff! Dining near the hearth is a grand idea. The dogs are already over there waiting for you, and the fire is just right. Enjoy the changing of the season.

My Perfect Pairing: Fritz Haag Brauneberger Juffer Sonnenuhr Riesling Auslese

From my notes: *Heady yet innocent scent of a clean dairy barn, and at the same time my art class from grade school, dusty and brimming with creativity, flavors from minerals to apple fritters, and later Honeycomb cereal with milk!*

Inspiration From My Notes: For The Love Of Grandmothers

The love between mother and daughter is forever, and the lessons handed down are profound. And it makes sense that insights passed on from grandmother to granddaughter would be intensified. My family is no exception. And on it goes like this from one to the next.

With a bit of mindfulness you can elevate your chores into the time of your life. The decadence of doing is powerful and rewarding.

Everyday Indulgence: Heavenly Fruitcake

My mother's mother taught me about tenacity and the benefits of working hard. Throughout my growing up, she toiled long hours as a baker for a local institution of a restaurant in our town. I remember the swirling, steamy kitchen of her world and the intoxicating and singular scent of her signature sweet rolls, created in a never-ending neat and tidy stream of delicious knots, each roll a carbon copy of the one before and after it. I marveled at her skill and longed to create as she did.

This is another one of her specialties: fruitcake. It takes a few days to prepare, as you make your own candied fruits. After that, a once-a-week ritualistic bath of brandy or rum renders these dense, fruit-laden cakes irresistible (and anything but dry). For the best (and most decadent) results, douse the cake for three or four weeks before slicing.

Ingredients

¾ cup turbinado sugar

1 cup amber agave nectar, divided into two ½-cup portions, plus 2 tablespoons

2 15-ounce cans sliced pineapple, no sugar added, drained

1 ½ cups pineapple juice, reserved from the canned pineapple

2 15-ounce cans sweet cherries, drained

¼ cup cherry juice, reserved from the canned cherries

2 ¼ cups chopped dates

½ cup brandy, plus more for basting

½ cup Bourbon

Splash orange juice

5 cups coarsely chopped nuts

1 ½ cups butter

1 ½ cups sugar

5 large eggs

3 teaspoons vanilla extract

½ cup plus 3 ½ cups sifted all-purpose flour

4 teaspoons baking powder

1 teaspoon salt

1 teaspoon freshly ground nutmeg

1 teaspoon ginger

4 cups coarsely chopped nuts

Rum for basting

Start by hanging some bird feeders in your favorite plum tree. The first few years you may not see many birds. Be patient. The birds will come. Eventually, they will find you and when they do, they will tell all of their friends. Busy bird-feeders are like well-established restaurants:

consistent. Grandmothers have the best bird feeders because they have been feeding the same birds the same way (usually well) for years. The birds like that.

Once you have made many bird friends and your feeders are flush with cheerful activity, and usually just as the sky threatens to snow, it is a good time to get to the business of making fruitcake. Have some tea, rest a bit and take a look out there; have they come? Aren't they beautiful the way they flip and dive around each other, so bold that even your presence doesn't send them flitting up and away?

Yes, it's time to make the cakes.

In a large, wide pan, stir the turbinado sugar, ½ cup agave nectar and pineapple juice over medium-high heat until it bubbles to a boil. Note the incredible quality, the gorgeous jewel-like translucence of the sugar in the amber as you mix—something like the tips of feathers on a hummingbird's wings. Slowly it dissolves, and the soft boil is ready to receive the pineapple slices. Turn the heat to simmer and let them go for about 25 minutes, until the edges of the fruit start to become transparent. Remove the golden pineapple slices, and set them aside on a plate to dry. Add the cherries to the same pan along with 1/4 cup of the cherry juice and 2 more tablespoons agave nectar. Return to boil, reduce heat and simmer another 25 minutes. Remove the plump cherries, draining them on a separate plate. (I like to save the leftover glaze as it makes a great substitute for sugar cubes in cocktails that call for the flavor of cherry as well.)

In a glass bowl, stir together the brandy, Bourbon and remaining ½ cup agave nectar. Add the chopped dates, stir to coat, and set aside. You will be stirring this bowl of dates each day for up to three days. During this time, your pineapple and cherries will be finishing off their candying process out in the open on the counter.

In the coming days, you will be ready to make the cakes. Make sure your birds are fed first, then get to baking. Preheat the oven to 275° F. Line four 8"x4 ½" x 2 1/2" baking pans with parchment paper cut into strips to fit the width of the bottom of the pan, greased with shortening or butter on the loaf side and with the ends extending (they will serve as handles for you to remove the loaf later).

Dust the fruits with about ½ cup of flour. Cream together the butter and sugar until fluffy, add the eggs and vanilla, and mix well. In a separate bowl, sift remaining flour, baking powder, salt and spices. Add to egg mixture and blend well.

Coarsely chop the pineapple, roughly into quarters is fine, and add them and the chopped nuts to the mixture, blending it all together with your hands. Add the dates, and continue mixing with your hands a few times. Add the cherries; they are the most delicate, so add them last and carefully. The dough will be sticky now, so using your hands is necessary: Grandma says, "When you are a baker, you can use your hands." Distribute the fruits evenly, without overmixing. Turn the mix into the prepared pans and bake on a center rack for about 2 hours, or until a wooden pick comes out clean. Place a pie tin of water on a lower rack to keep the loaves moist during baking.

Once done, cool the cakes, and wrap them in cheesecloth and foil. Before sealing the foil, use a brush to paint the tops of each loaf with brandy or rum, using about ¼ cup per loaf. Store the loaves in the refrigerator, painting their tops daily for a week, then once a week thereafter, keep them a total of three or four weeks before slicing—or before sending to your granddaughter 2,600 miles away who watches the post daily in anticipation of their arrival each year at just about the same time. Likewise she waits for the birds and their songs to return, with excitement, delight and gratitude each year.

My Perfect Pairing: Disznókő, Tokaji Aszú 5 Puttonyos

From my notes: *Clean, beautiful, wonderful honey! Yes! It is true, actually smells just like grandma's fruitcake!*

Everyday Indulgence: Slovenian Potica

My joyful Slovenian grandmother taught my sister and I as little girls to love many things. Above all else, to enjoy the moment in the real world here and now. No fake reality for us, just nature, the garden, our imaginations and two well-loved banana-seat bicycles. The television was turned off sometime in early May and we were kicked out of the house until the snow returned to spend our days playing in the grassy yard, riding our bikes or helping in the endless sea of undulating green that was the beloved vegetable and flower garden.

In the summer, my grandmother worked hard and created daily in her sunny, cheerful kitchen. The basement root cellar was stocked floor to ceiling with every imaginable canned good—which she produced with her own two hands on her sturdy gas stove. She made these things all day long in cauldrons so tall I couldn't see their tops, which bubbled and steamed starting in August, and all the way into October some years, if the yield was heavy and good. That dusty underground room held gem-colored jams and jellies, rows of thick, rich, speckled spaghetti sauces and bright jars of sweet and sour pickles that made my mouth water simply by holding them in my hands. I respected her dedication and adored her work. At the end of each canning day, she cleaned the kitchen and somehow produced a complete meal as well—featuring the latest root-cellar addition, often still a bit warm from the processing.

The fall brought apple butter festivals and Gram's plump, rustic berry pies cooling on windowsills the old-fashioned way. We played in piles of leaves, helped with her harvest, and added more layers of sweaters as the days demanded. Often we kept our sun-bleached summer dresses on under the sweaters and over the top of our long underwear or jeans, in a defiant last stand against the oncoming coldness. We knew our days outside were numbered, but another paradise awaited inside the warm, cozy house.

In winter we watched Gram flip through the endless cookbooks that she kept stacked next to her favorite chair, wondering what on earth the strange Slovenian words were saying to her. Now that TV was allowed back on, she would often shout to us for a pencil if she wanted to note down what wonder the folks on the morning program were preparing. We knew enough to understand that she was looking for treat recipes for holiday goodies or just plain-old cold, blustery January, which was a fine thing in our housebound opinion.

Baking was its own special sport, and I think now that we may have loved this best. While fixing herself a cup of coffee and planning the day's kitchen mischief, Gram would dial in and crank up what she referred to as the "jives" on the little, rounded, white clock-radio that sat on the Formica countertop. The tune of "Tennessee Waltz" or "Red River Valley" was always a welcome inspiration to our dishes, and if the DJ wasn't playing those songs, well then we sang them ourselves at her prompting. It was often encouraged that my sister and I accompany whatever music was playing with some wild dancing around the warm kitchen. And then the baking began. Cakes, kuchens, cookies, strudels and the most adored, potica. She made it so special and fun and never discouraged little hands from helping. She cared much more about the process and the lesson than whether the final outcome was lopsided or a bit rough around the edges. Gram believed in the decadence of doing.

Sweet dough rose in the huge metal bowl she called a *sklada* (which was big enough to double as a sled for us, and we used it as such) and then was rolled out paper-thin over the entire kitchen table on top of a floured cotton tablecloth. Various fillings, from crispy bacon (yes! cracklin strudel!) to sweet cherry or spiced apple slices, were carefully smoothed out on top, and then, after a short snowstorm of sugar, magically the whole project was rolled from one end to the other with the assistance of the tablecloth (and two pairs of little girl hands). The lumpy log was transformed in the dark oven to a layered slice of sweet or savory heaven, perfuming the house with its irresistible aromas (later I would find this exact scent in many of my favorite wine bouquets). All of the baking was like this: theatrical, earthy, laced heavily with the rituals of our tradition and heritage. This spoke to the deepest parts of my little girl artist soul, and the seed of decadent doing was planted for good.

Nothing puts me into a holiday mood more that the serious business of making *potica*. It is involved and laborious, with its important steps and slow pace. But it is wrapped so tightly inside the loving memories of my now gone grandmother that I continue the tradition and make it each year. Sometimes I have to leave out the salt because my tears fall in the bowl when I hear her in my mind reading the recipe to me while I work. This is a sweet potica recipe, but I have had wonderful luck with a savory pork belly potica as well, based on an ocvirkova (crackling) potica recipe handed down from my great grandma Debelak, Vita's beloved mother. Carry on I say.

Ingredients

Dough

1 yeast cake or 1 package of yeast

1 ½ cups lukewarm milk

3 tablespoons sugar

½ cup melted butter

½ pint full-fat sour cream

1 cup sugar

1 tablespoon salt

3 whole eggs plus an extra yolk

8 cups flour

Crumble yeast into warm milk with 3 tablespoons sugar and whip up to a little froth. Set aside and let stand. Mix melted butter, sour cream, sugar, salt and eggs (plus the extra yolk) in a large bowl. Once combined, add the yeast mixture to this bowl and lightly stir to integrate. Add about 8 cups of flour just until dough holds a form. Turn on board and kneed to a soft round of dough. Place in a greased bowl, and let dough raise to double in size.

Filling

1 cup milk

½ pound honey

1 ½ pound nuts, ground (good thing for the kids to do) walnuts are best

¼ pound butter, melted

½ cup sugar

1 tablespoon black walnut extract

Rind of 1 lemon, grated

1 whole egg, beaten

Boil milk, add honey, nuts, butter, sugar, walnut extract and lemon rind. On top of a floured cotton tablecloth, roll dough ¼-inch thick on the kitchen table. Dough will cover a large area. Spread filling on top evenly. Roll, and coil on a greased baking sheet, set aside to rise again for about an hour. Brush top with whole beaten egg and bake at 325° F for 1 hour.

When the whole thing comes out, and the kitchen is all clean and shining again, put up your feet and have some nice hot coffee and a thick slice of this delicious, rare treat.

My Perfect Pairing: Harlan The Maiden Napa Proprietary Red

From my notes: *Caramelized fennel, dates and sausages, delicious wine this smells just like White Bros. Bakery. Gram, I miss you!*

Love Letters: Polkas And The Love Of Snow

Salute.

I'm not sure why I had to tell you this except I wanted you to know.

Thanks for telling me.

I am a very busy boy in the world.

You are a very busy boy in many worlds. What type of music do you play?

French and Italian film music and polkas whenever asked—accordion is what I have been playing the most of late.

I am Slovenian and Hungarian gypsy. I adore the accordion. I find it as sexy as the cello (which I find very sexy) and I must have known that about you, in my collective gypsy memory. I ripped my stockings once right up the back of one calf, during a feverish polka in a town hall. And French and Italian film music ... which? I must have some immediately. My favorite movie ever is a 1990 French film. The music is unbelievable. It is called Mazeppa. Do you know it? It is my film. I watched it once and took notes and drew things from it in the pitch dark. It is about horses and a painter and an equestrian circus like no other.

I am going, will be gone soon. I am sure it will be spectacular there with the snow.

Thank you for finding me. I needed another artist to talk to.

Travel well, and look for my constellation, up there, watching.

P.s. I would like to know what time of day were you born, how you take your coffee, when did you start to play the guitar, and why?

What makes you and your family unique? What simple yet decadent traditions did you grow up with that you have forgotten? What did they feel like? Can you try them again?

My Perfect Pairing: Le Salette Amarone della Valpolicella Classico La Marega

From my notes: *Prunes, figs, raisins, almonds, Valentine's Day message hearts, confectionary candy, powdered sugar jelly donut, watermelon*

Inspiration From My Notes: Winter Evening Barn Chores

Feeling sleepy-dreamy to the tune of a haunting accordion—the moon has been amazing lately—with a beautiful moonrise last night and awesome cold, bright nights. The weather has been very wintery and gray, and I love it. I cannot wait to go to the snow, I miss it so much. Cold, icy, frozen world snaps into view … a memory of barn chores in winter.

Wearing so many clothes—three pairs of pants, four shirts, a coat, gloves—and going out into the frosty night to take care of the animals. The barn warm with horse breath and smelling of hay and pony fur. Throwing feed and fragrant alfalfa, and breaking ice and sloshing half-frozen water on the snowy ground, and new water, steamy, and the never-ending dance under the hose, draining it each night so that we would have water the next day. There were many winterland adventures on my pony, Brownie, with our little sled decorated with ribbons and bits of garland. Delivering cookies to neighbors, especially I remember those times, and her fur and her bells and her little hooves and gray fetlocks. I miss her still. Bells.

Sleep now. xo

Find the warmth inside the coldness. Is it a cheerful color, a single candle flame, a kind gesture toward someone close by or far away?

Everyday Indulgence: Russian Tea Cakes

The sound of tiny hooves on frozen ground kept perfect time with the jingle of the harness as Brownie trotted out smartly ahead of us. We whizzed along the snow in our sled hitched behind her, level with her low hocks, skimming along the hard-packed snowy street, empty of traffic. Behind me, my wisp of a little sister, small but puffy with the costume of snowplay, holding brightly wrapped plates of carefully crafted Christmas cookies. We were on a delivery route and I was driving, thick reins soft from years of use and saddle soap held loosely in my mittened hands. We knew as we delivered goodies, plate by plate to surprised neighbors, what was waiting. When we were done, and Brownie was groomed and kissed several times and had her marshmallows and a million pats and was resting in the barn with the other horses methodically munching sweet hay from her little bin, we would be at our own table sampling the latest in the holiday lineup paired perfectly with steaming hot chocolate or ice cold milk. None of them compared to our Russian Tea Cakes.

Ingredients

1 cup cold, unsalted butter	2 ½ cups all-purpose flour
½ cup powdered sugar	¾ cup walnuts, ground or finely chopped by hand
1 teaspoon vanilla	
½ teaspoon black walnut extract	½ teaspoon salt

With the Harry Simone Chorale pumping away at Little Drummer Boy in the room next door, the cat climbing the Christmas tree and your little sisters bouncing off the walls with the excitement of the season, it is not always easy to concentrate on the serious task of making Russian Tea Cakes for your neighbors. Somehow Mom would get us focused and on board, especially for the fun job of rolling each little cake in a double bath of powdered sugar at the end. To make the cakes, well, I think she did most of the heavy lifting so they came out magically delicious. Though the process is simple, a few tweaks will leave you with tough cookies, and I don't know anyone who thinks that is, um, anything but tough cookies.

Preheat the oven to 400° F. In a mixing bowl, cream the butter with a hand mixer and add in the sugar and extracts. Mix the flour, nuts and salt together briefly in a separate bowl, and then add to the cream mixture using the mixer. I find that this recipe is a lot like making pie dough; you want to keep it cool for crisp yet flaky cookies. Once the dough is holding together on its own, which doesn't take long, stop mixing. Send someone to retrieve the cat from the tree and turn on the outdoor lighting display. How pretty!

Form the dough into ½-inch balls and place on an ungreased cookie sheet about 2 inches apart. (You can line the sheet with parchment paper if you have it handy.) Bake for 10 minutes, until the cakes just turn brown. While still warm, roll them in powdered sugar to coat, then gently move them to a rack to cool. Once they are cool (are there any left?), roll them once more in powdered sugar. When they look like plump little snowmen bellies, your work is done. Now go stretch out under the Christmas tree with your head near the bowl of water she's sitting in, and admire the lights from a new angle.

My Perfect Pairing: E. Guigal Côtes du Rhône

From my notes: *Rose petal, butter cookies, walking through a hyacinth garden—but not putting your nose down into the flowers*

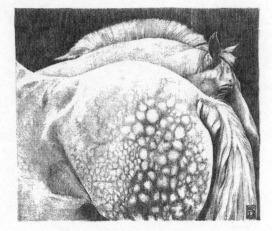

110

DECADENT INTERCOURSES

Sharing decadence is one of the best ways to experience it. It matters not whether the exchange is spoken word, the silent wrapping of beautiful legs around a hot powerful horse, or the private soul talk between a painter and his subject. There are a million ways to make love.

Inspiration From My Notes: Up On Four Legs

There were always horses.

The first, a big black-and-white stud under my mother and me while she and I still shared a heartbeat. Then, the pony she trusted me on—almost alone—when I was just old enough to saddle a pony myself. When that little brown pony had a little Appaloosa filly out of that black-and-white stud, that filly became my muse. She taught me so much; so slow and undetected until things were just right, training her with Mom when I was about nine, after filly and I both grew up a little.

Then there was my fiery red mare, full of sass, who threw a leggy copper stud colt one year. He would become my horse from the moment his mother rejected him, a horse I would, much later, ride on freezing cold nights, alone together, fusing like two chunks of red hot metal in the icy, snowy night—minds as one, learning how to dance up on four legs.

A buckskin girl, partner in crime, trotted me all over creation and knew the way to my boyfriend's house by heart in the dark. A silky purple wisp of a rose gray Arabian, who could move sideways just as fast as he could go forward, taught me about perfect sensitivity in every moment.

And now there is only one, speckled delicate as the thin shells of eggs. All the others prepared me for the most divine ride of my life to date— the girl no one wanted, or could ride very well, because she was too confident and unwilling to give up anything, not one thing. This mare has taught me more about life than I could ever have imagined. She brings me to my knees and makes me cry instant, hard tears with her giant, gorgeous heart, once cold and stormy, now open and so huge it pulses out and pushes up through her, through the saddle and right into my own. We fly like a centaur, my starry archer and I, through the perfectly blue-black sky.

There were always horses. There will always be horses.

Responsibility, sensitivity, appreciation of beauty, creativity and profound, elegant respect. My life with horses has taught me more than I can describe. Above all is the importance of learning to share things deeply—it's one of the most decadent things you can do with your time.

Everyday Indulgence: Slow Beef Stew

A good beef stew is hard to beat, especially since most of the work is done without your help. This is my take on the classic. I have simplified wherever possible, as I feel decadence is delicious food, not fussy food.

Ingredients

3 to 4 pound round roast

Half a bunch of celery

5 big carrots

12 golden fingerling potatoes, cut in halves or thirds

1 shallot

4 cloves garlic

Spelt flour, enough for dredging

Coarse salt and fresh pepper

1 teaspoon dried thyme; less if using fresh thyme from your garden

2 cups beef stock

Finish work early and plan to head to the barn for the rest of the afternoon. Chop the celery and carrots into good-sized chunks, slice the shallot, and mince the garlic well. Cut the meat into evenly sized cubes, and dredge them in spelt flour sprinkled with salt and pepper. In a large soup pot, warm some olive oil, add the shallots, garlic and salt and pepper. Once the garlic starts to crisp, add the dried thyme or a little chopped fresh thyme. Drop in the cubes of dredged beef, browning evenly on all sides but not cooking through. Move the browned meat to a plate as you work quickly. (You might even make a little coffee now for your Thermos, to take with you out the door when you leave in a moment.) Once all the meat is browned, reduce the heat, and add all the ingredients back into the pot, including the vegetables, seasonings and beef stock. Bring it all to a boil, then drop the heat down very, very low, to just a simmer. Make sure you have enough stock in the pot if you plan to let it simmer while you slip outside. I like to add a cup of cold water so that the whole thing can cook down over the course of the next few hours while I ride away the stress of the world, returning to the kitchen tired, sore and happy as hell that I had the good sense to make this lovely dish ahead of time.

My Perfect Pairing: Kiplinger Syrah

From my notes: *Classic, earthy, ripe and delicious. Big, rich fruit, molasses, love this, now anise! Delightful!*

Love Letters: The Real Thing

So let's just keep telling stories to each other and be beautiful together. Opening your words is like walking through the doors of the world's finest art museums ... and I feel like I am the only one there. If you enjoy that, then keep writing.

I lived in Amsterdam one autumn. The air was moist and gray very often, and tall strange buildings built of brick lined the canal-snaked streets. Those streets became a maze of wet ribbons with the rain, and I rode my bicycle all over that city upon them, alone. I ached for a man in my life, and I found one. He spoke to me through brushstrokes and color, in paintings that quivered on still walls with the energy of their creation. Under a Dutch moon hidden by thin clouds, Van Gogh seduced me. He was my ghost lover for several months. I felt his pain and I wanted to throw all of the strangers out of our museum so that we could be alone. Instead I sat there for hours and recreated his works in my own sketchbooks as careful as a lover to the details he instructed. The obsession went on for quite some time. In fact, it took a threesome with Franz Marc and Egon Scheile four years later to finally get me over him.

Now you tell me one. My tears are dry.

Have a day. Make it great. xo

My Perfect Pairing: Screaming Eagle

From my notes: *This is incredible. The nose is like Christmas, with venison and sweet red cabbage, amazing, and four big bunches of roses in the nose*

Inspiration From My Notes: Potatoes Of The Oven

The phone just rang. It was Guiseppe. He has invited me to dinner at his flat tonight. He was breathy and hot on the phone as my flatmate and I crowded together listening to him. He said, "Sherri, Sherri, I have one question to ask to you," and his imperfect English in his gorgeous Italian accent was so damn sexy. "Do you like (long pause), potatoes?" I almost fainted. She and I looked at each other and died laughing without making a sound. I recovered and replied, "Si, Guiseppe, I like potatoes." He went on, "Oh that is so good. I'm making patate al forno (potatoes of the oven) for you tonight, special, and I am so, so happy that you like … potatoes." So was I. He knew how to treat a girl, realmente (indeed).

An Italian accent transformed the humble potato into absolute decadence for me. Celebrate with your friends and the simple becomes sublime.

Everyday Indulgence: Patate Al Forno

In my little corner of the world, nothing is more decadent than the simplicity of a perfectly roasted potato kissed with garlic, salt and crispy rosemary. Fittingly, this recipe is great with Perfectly Roasted Chicken (see "Discovering Decadence"), but beware that the effect on your diners could be life-altering.

Ingredients

Small potatoes (redskin, yellow or new potatoes, whatever you like) chopped into 1-inch cubes, equivalent of a generous handful per person

Olive oil

Coarse salt

Fresh pepper

3 cloves garlic, minced

Several branches fresh rosemary, coarsely chopped, or about 1 tablespoon dried rosemary

Fresh sage (optional); same proportion as the rosemary

Ready? Preheat oven to 450° F. Toss all ingredients in a bowl, and swirl them around until potato chunks are well-coated. Spread potatoes in a single layer on a baking sheet, and roast for about 30 minutes, turning potatoes few times. Alora! Stupende!

My Perfect Pairing: Refosco Dal Peduncolo Rosso Vigneto Montsclapade

From my notes: *Gorgeous color, powerfully elegant, ripe berries, toasted pine nuts, fruity pebbles and craisins, wild berries; love this wine*

Inspiration From My Notes: The Pick Up

Back from two days on the road with my lover. Fast trip to pick up paintings from the gallery—very fun drive there, twisting through the redwoods and snaking up valleys. In a whirlwind we stuffed the car full of art and left for the cabin in the woods—to a vintage postcard of a place on some lake, in the middle of nowhere in Oregon. And we had the very best time. In the car on the drive we talked so much! We got all hot and crazed, laughing, we had to stop to make love furiously—very exciting!

We arrived at our little cabin, but first slipped in for thick steaks and creamy baked potatoes just before they closed the restaurant there. Then gin at the bar, sitting on high stools, swirled into each other, my legs draped over his, forehead to forehead—just talking, talking, talking with so much passion about everything under the moon. They finally kicked us out and back to our cabin in the still, quiet night where we made the loudest, rowdiest love ever—crying out and carrying on like a pair of wolves—only to realize around 4 a.m. that we had left all the windows wide open, no doubt broadcasting our every move to the hundred other campers at the otherwise silent lake that night. We fell asleep in each others arms with my head pressed to his shoulder and his heart beating strong under my ear, and I knew I was exactly where I needed to be. Breakfast was interesting. Inspiration everywhere and all around.

If you are worried about making noise, you most likely need to make more. Cry out.

Everyday Indulgence: Filets With Wild Mushrooms (And Baked Potatoes)

Because we sell red wine all over the country, we often find ourselves paying our respects at the steak houses that carry them. The simplicity of these classic menus never takes away from the decadence of these meals. Pairing good steak with deep red wine is a natural. Some things never go out of style.

If you are feeling ambitious, make these baked potatoes about an hour ahead of your dinner so that they are ready to go with the steaks. If not, the steaks are just as good with fresh asparagus, wilted spinach or a decadent mac and cheese.

Ingredients

2 large Idaho potatoes

Coarse salt and fresh pepper

Cold water

2 6-ounce filet mignons, rinsed and patted dry

¾ pounds cremini or button mushrooms, sliced

Olive oil

3 thick slices bacon, diced

1 large onion, diced

You have been hiking all day and feel your iron levels may be dipping. Hmmm. A thick, juicy steak and a bottle of lush red wine are just what the doctor ordered. (Bonus if you can get him to come over and make this for you.)

Get a head start on the potatoes. Preheat the oven to 325° F, poke a few holes in the potatoes, sprinkle them with water, salt and pepper and wrap them in foil. Now, load them in the oven while you work on the Doctor. I mean, his meat. I mean, the *filets*. (Well you do have a little time before you really need to get cooking on the rest of this recipe—it's your night, you decide.) At the very least, pick out a nice Cabernet Sauvignon from the cellar and get it decanted.

Rub the filets with a bit of olive oil and the sliced garlic, salt and pepper, and set them off to the side. In a large, dry skillet, sweat the sliced mushrooms. Let them caramelize slightly, and reduce down just a bit. In the meantime, in a second sauté pan, add olive oil (about 2 to 3 tablespoons, or enough to coat the bottom of the pan well). Add the bacon and fry it, rendering the fat. Remove the fried bacon and set it aside. Now would be a good time to try that wine (fyi, there is no rule saying you can't pair it with some of that hot bacon). Now, add the onions to the oil and bacon fat and sauté them until translucent. Once they are ready, mix together the mushrooms, bacon and onions in one of the pans. Set this aside with the heat off.

Have the Doc set the table, light a few candles and find some appropriate music (anything from Van Morrison to Paul Butterfield will work for this one, or have him surprise you).

Turn the oven up to broil. If the potatoes are close to done, simply move them to the farthest rack from the broiler flame; if they are done, remove them from the oven entirely. Time your steaks; they will take 5 to 7 minutes per side depending on how thick they are and how you like your meat cooked. Place the meat under the broiler, and set the timer for 5 minutes. Turn the steaks after 5 to 7 again, depending on your taste. Broil for another 5 to 7 minutes. Remove the filets from the broiler and let them rest for a moment while you reheat the mushrooms and onions, stirring a bit to reunite them all.

Now (wow that smells good; you feel your iron levels rising already) plate the steaks and pile them with mushrooms and onions. Slice open the potatoes and pinch them puffy, adding butter and sour cream. Simple indulgence. And doctor's orders, after all.

My Perfect Pairing: Groth Cabernet Sauvignon Reserve 1985

From my notes: *Baked blackberry cobbler, chocolate mint cake, herbs toasted in the oven, pale sage, rose, beet warm from the ground, hot tar, saddle leather and horse blankets, tea rose, sugar beet on palate, with aged balsamic, perfect balance, long, lush finish and still black cherry fruit and the crust of a crème brûlée*

Inspiration From My Notes: Musings Of Mine

Tonight I watched a beautiful film. It made me cry. It made me think about life. What do I want to look back on when I am ready to die and remember with fondness? What do I want my life to look like? Who do I want to be and become, and what legacy leave?

A painter. I want to give my art to the world to make people happy and bring them light. I want to give gifts of beauty and timelessness and transcendence. I want to always embrace the responsibility of making art. I want to take those opportunities and not take them for granted.

A lover. I want to love well. To give my whole heart and soul to those around me. And invite in those who will return the favor.

I want to always remember and honor my past. My garden life with Gramma and the simplicity of that. The goodness and the love there. I feel a burning need to somehow interpret that in my work—I think because to me it is beauty—it is the emotion of beauty—and I want to manifest that emotion in my paintings.

I want to grow good gardens and eat good food. Drink good wine and make good love. Celebrate the seasons and work hard. Enjoy things like good air and soft grass, warm sand, sweaty tired lover's skin, salty horses strong under me, red lipstick on salsa night. I want to look back and remember richness of experience and realness—not all work and fear. I would say that I feel I have lived a full life already. My goodness, what I have done! Sometimes I wish I could have done less. Sometimes I wish I wasn't so driven, that just being would be enough. So I will try to find balance. Life versus the pursuit of life. It is all so strange. And wonderful, too.

Simply acknowledging your true self and what moves you allows your soul to indulge in some small way each day. In the end, it adds up to a lifetime of commitment to yourself and to your dreams that you can be content with.

Everyday Indulgence: (The Best) Chicken Soup (Ever)

For me in my kitchen there is nothing like languishing all day over a rich, deep pot of fragrant soup. The evolution of it is at once quite simple yet infinitely complex. A day of adjusting, building, reducing and revising. Not many soups reach the heights of the humble and remarkable chicken soup. Mine is built on the classic recipe. But it does have a few additions you may not have tried. The best thing you can do? Use what you have and add extra love.

My chicken soup is on the rich side. If you are some kind of purist and like a cleaner soup, ditch some of the herbs.

Ingredients

1 fresh, organic chicken (or a whole leftover roast chicken)

6 cloves garlic, minced

1 large sweet onion, chopped

1 ½ bunches celery, chopped, divided into 2 equal portions

12 large carrots, peeled and sliced, divided into 2 equal portions

1 cube chicken bouillon, or 1 teaspoon of the paste variety

Worcestershire sauce

1 bunch rosemary

2 bunches rainbow chard

Bay leaf

Coarsely grated Parmesan cheese

Rise early to the sound of a rainstorm. Make yourself a great cup of coffee and put on your galoshes. Walk the dog through the raindrops. On your way back inside, grab a handful of rosemary and two bunches of rainbow chard from your garden. Inside, turn up the heat for a bit (the dog looks cold) and put your apron on.

In your largest soup pot, place the chicken, garlic, onion, half the carrots and celery, 6 cups of water and all the seasonings; reserve the chard. Bring the pot to a boil, then reduce to a simmer. Tilt the lid to let steam escape, and go work on something else for about an hour. You can turn the heater down now too. The soup should be steaming up the windows at this point.

When you begin to smell something divine, go check on it. After about 3 hours with a raw chicken or one and a half with a cooked one, the bird will be ready to give up. Pull it out and let it cool so you can remove the meat from the bones. While you're deboning the chicken, parboil, in a separate pot, the remaining carrots and celery (add the celery after the carrots have had about 5 minutes of boiling). This is your pretty set of vegetables.

Transfer the chicken meat back to the stock, and adjust the seasonings. Depending on the contents of your pantry, add a starch: egg noodles, barley pearls or wild rice. Any of these items will add earthy dimension. Omitting them is also an option. You are really at liberty to make up your own rules with soup, and there isn't much that can result in disaster at this point. The only hard rules are taste often, bask in the steam and delicious warmth of your kitchen, sink into the process but don't overthink it. While the starch cooks, chiffonade your chard into pretty strips and add to the pot along with the parboiled celery and carrots. Adjust the seasonings again, as you like them.

Serve in big bowls, with a dusting of grated cheese. Fill mason jars with any leftovers and surprise sick friends with wellness, or well friends with a night off. Be prepared to invest in a second soup pot once folks taste your handiwork.

My Perfect Pairing: GKG Cabernet Sauvignon

From my notes: *Lush jam, balanced, red velvet cake, all pencil lead and Pacific sunsets. Happy Birthday, Mr. G*

Inspiration From My Notes:
Steamywarmcandleliteveningreadingsleepingdreaming

tonight
slipping into the shadow of a castle
a taste of opus 36 and then entertaining and now a bath
more wine and the book I am reading
the tao of equus
this painter needs a day of painting, but tomorrow is Monday
and I wonder why you are driving so much
what are you doing all those days on the road?
what do you think about?

the bath is ready
steamywarmcandleliteveningreadingsleepingdreaming
goodnight

Baths are decadent, light bulbs are not. Shut them off, light some candles and slip in. Bubbles optional;, I prefer mine in a glass.

My Perfect Pairing: Dow's Port 1948

From my notes: *So youthful, like new skin and fresh flowers, argyle and peat*

DECADENT JOURNEYS

I have had the pleasure and the good fortune to travel to many amazing places in my life thus far. I left home early and found my way in the world, which may have been my most rewarding journey, even though it was less than 15 miles in length. Big adventures to places far away have always enticed me, and giving in to their call has never let me down. Experiencing another place is a reminder to find delight in open eyes—unveil things familiar yet made new while taking place against a different background. See how a sunrise, a little bird bathing or even the light on the face of your longtime lover takes on a fresh dimension when you slip into a new time zone.

Inspiration From My Notes: Friesland Is A Province In The North Of The Netherlands

Driving through soft misty twilight along a tree-lined road, gray branches overhead reaching across to each other. Two horses, giant and black, stand side by side softly biting necks in the dim distant light from faraway farmhouses. Friesians! Black against silvery gray horizon. Houses big and low with pointed rooftops are like the spines of a great dinosaur asleep under the soft sand. A forest of trees huddled together against the wind still smelling of the old sea that the IJ remembers so well ...

Can you drive somewhere and discover something new before sundown?

Everyday Indulgence: Hélène's Quiche

I have a friend who has chickens and ducks. I buy eggs from her often and this is one of my favorite uses for those beautiful little ovals that decorate my refrigerator in such a charming way. This recipe is inspired by the many wonderful quiches I made with Hélène in Durgerdam during chilly days in the Netherlands.

Crust

1 ½ cups flour

1 stick salted butter (½ cup)

1 teaspoon fine salt

Approximately 3 tablespoons very cold water, to form dough

Filling

½ medium onion

2 shallots

1 cup diced bacon (about ½ pound)

1 cup diced cremini mushrooms

Splash of Sherry for deglazing

1 generous cup shredded Swiss, Edam, or Gouda cheese

5 duck eggs

1 ½ cups heavy cream

Whole fresh nutmeg for grating

Coarse salt

White pepper

Few things are finer than the scent of sizzling bacon. Its perfume can coax even the coldest camping nose out of a snow-dusted sleeping bag for breakfast during hunting season. Admittedly, I do not often make quiche while camping, but this would be a perfectly portable do-ahead dish if one were going to be in need of decadent fortification while out in the wild for a spell. Yes, wild men eat quiche and yes, you can reheat it on a camp stove quite successfully. But first for the civilized part, which starts with bacon.

In a medium sauté pan, cook the chopped bacon until crisp, rendering the fat in a glistening golden pool (watch for spitting!). I like to use bacon "ends," which are basically the mismatched trimmings from those nice tidy packages you are used to seeing on the shelf. The ends are meatier, thicker, and funkier and work well chopped into bites. Once the bacon is crisp, remove it from the pan, and brown the onions in the rendered fat. In a second dry pan, sweat the diced mushrooms with salt until their liquid gives itself up; keep cooking over medium heat until they almost dry back out, then at the last minute, deglaze them with a nice splash of Sherry. Mix well, remove from heat and set aside.

I like to use my food processor for the dough, but it can be done by hand. If using a processor, set up with the pastry blade, and add the flour, salt and then the butter in slices on top of it. Pulse until it turns crumbly, and then add ice water a tablespoon at a time until the dough forms into a ball.

If you are doing it by hand, use a big bowl and layer the ingredients the same way, cutting the butter in with a pastry blender. Again, when it crumbles, mix by hand, adding water, until the dough forms. Either way at this point, pat it into a ball (but do not overwork the dough).

Next, press the dough in sections into the bottom and sides of your quiche pan (yes, the type where the bottom comes out; it's ideal and worth the investment) to about a ¼-inch thickness all around. Bring the crust's sides up higher than the pan's, and press into a smooth lip. Prick the shell with a fork all over, and brush with the sunny yolk of one of your duck eggs. Bake it at 375° F for about 10 minutes, until golden brown.

The egg mixture is simply 4 whole eggs, heavy cream, a nice grating of fresh nutmeg (I keep whole nutmeg in the kitchen at all times for good luck, and quiche apparently) and salt and white pepper. Whisk the eggs, and then whisk in the cream and seasonings until you have a slightly frothy mixture. Place the bacon, mushrooms and cheese in the baked shell, and pour the egg mix on top of it all. Bake this delight in the oven for about 30 minutes, until the egg sets.

Another option is make several quiches at once, with different fillings. Simply double the ingredients for the dough and egg mixture, but try another flavor for the second quiche. I like sausage and sautéed red and gold peppers with fennel salt. A nice vegetarian option is wilted spinach and diced summer squash, sautéed before being added. Don't forget a cup of cheese per quiche. Split the egg mix, and bake several quiches together. Use your imagination (or clean out your refrigerator) and come up with your own creation.

A nice compliment to the rich quiche warm from the oven is a few simple cool leaves of butter lettuce dressed only with a drizzle of walnut oil and a hint of sea salt. Unless of course you awake just before dawn with stars fading over your snow camp and enjoy a slice out of hand while still in your warm sleeping bag. Ah, decadence knows no rules.

My Perfect Pairing: Christian Moreau Père & Fils Chablis

From my notes: *Buttered Saltines with Swiss cheese, lovely light and whispery hint of citrus. Nothing overpowers, everything one big balance*

Inspiration From My Notes: The Vortex To Infinity

One of my favorite views of the Napa Valley was discovered one particularly gorgeous, and important, early spring afternoon in the ethereal wake of a long, feverish night spent with a most amazing man. The air was clear and sunny—with bud break threatening to occur in the time it would take us to have lunch. After a brief attempt to dine in a large and busy restaurant where we were seated in some energetic vortex which left us both, at the very same moment, a breath away from fainting, my lover grabbed my hand and said we had to get out of this strange cosmic funnel.

Off we drove, up the Silverado Trail and east into a steep drive that wound up a short distance to a swanky, Dionysian sort of spot that he knew well. This luxury resort blankets the land like a silky spa robe dropped coyly on the hillside just between St. Helena and Rutherford. It has a fantastic restaurant with perfect food and fussy service, but he knew that the real draw was the view. Outside we went, through the little bar onto the rustic wooden deck. We sat there together, settled and solemn and quiet after our joint fainting spell, happy to be somewhere else, simply enjoying each other's presence and the freshness of spring in the air. Words were unnecessary. The view said it all, stretched out below all the way to what seemed like San Francisco, gorgeous vineyards and tree-lined side roads in a wine country quilt! We had apple tart and Champagne. A perfect pairing. A perfect day.

If you find yourself in a situation that is sucking the life out of you, know when to say enough is enough! A change of scenery is all you need to gain fresh perspective. Take some pillows outside and have dessert for dinner. Climb high somewhere and see what unfolds below.

Everyday Indulgence: Apple Tart

This is a pretty treat to make when your neighbor gives you a cheerful bowl of apples at harvesttime. Not overly sweet, it pairs as well with coffee as it does with Champagne. Use your best judgment.

Ingredients

3 large apples, peeled, cored and sliced

½ a whole fresh lemon

1 teaspoon cinnamon

1 tablespoon sugar

3 teaspoons vanilla salt, for sprinkling

Dough

2 cups sifted flour

3/4 cup cold butter (1½ sticks)

1 tablespoon sugar

⅓ cup cold water

Pinch of salt

2 eggs, separated, yolks reserved

Almond Paste Dough

2/3 cup almonds, roasted or raw

2/3 cup sugar

2 egg whites, reserved from ingredients above

I find that working with my hands helps clear my head when I have a decision weighing on my heart. The answers I need often appear halfway through the project. If you have a something pending and you need time to think, this easy apple tart is the perfect project. And it looks as good as it tastes.

Preheat the oven to 375° F. Next, ground yourself while peeling and coring the apples. Slice them in even crescents or neat rounds. Pay attention to their shapes; they will be the basis for your tart design later. (It will also give your conscious mind something to focus on so your gut can talk to the rest of your brain and give you the insight you seek.) Squeeze the juice of the lemon on top of the sliced apples, and toss to coat. The juice will keep them pearly white. Set aside.

In a food processor fitted with a pastry blade, combine the sifted flour, very cold sliced butter, 1 tablespoon sugar, ⅓ cup cold water and a pinch of salt. Pulse until a soft dough is formed. Do not overprocess the dough or it will become tough. Transfer it to the tart pan in sections, first forming the dough roughly into a ball and then simply using your hands to press it into the tart pan, creating a shell about ¼-inch thick all the way around. With a fork, prick the bottom of the crust, then paint the unbaked shell with the slightly beaten egg yolks. Bake the shell for about 10 minutes, until it starts to turn golden brown.

While the shell is in the oven, make the almond paste. No need to wash the food processor; just change the blade and scrape the sides clean. Combine the almonds, sugar and egg whites into a smooth paste. When the mesmerizing action stops (has your insight arrived yet?) fill the bottom of the golden crust with the almond paste. Sprinkle it with a bit of vanilla salt.

Stir the cinnamon and the remaining tablespoon of sugar into the apples, coating them nicely. Arrange them in a design on top of the almond paste (a spiral for crescents is nice or a flower shape for rounds works well), layering as you go and covering the entire almond base. Sprinkle a bit more vanilla salt on top, and bake for about 40 minutes, until the top is golden and a bit caramelized.

Still thinking? Close your eyes. Practice a few deep mind-cleansing breaths near the oven, taking in the sweet smell. Ah. Open your eyes and check on the progress. As the tart begins to glisten, there it is: the clarity your mind needed and the answer from your heart. Just in time for dessert.

My Perfect Pairing: Louis Roederer Brut Premier

From my notes: *The ocean! The sea! Like licking saltwater off your lover's warm skin*

Inspiration From My Notes: France Is A Very Sexy Place

We are now in France! Came by overnight ferry with our car. We are staying at the most gorgeous place, Villefranche de Lonchat. I'm at the window now with the beautiful view of the moon over the elegantly curved tile rooftops across the street. France is a very sexy place.

I think we have found the most perfect spot in the world. I wish we could live here! It is so peaceful, so relaxed, I love it all. Carrying baskets to the bread shop, wearing sundresses, eating outside, having only the barest of essentials of clothes, fluffy feather duvets, watching the full moon rise out of sight before you fall asleep. It is gorgeous, what more can I say?

I want to be out painting EVERYTHING! I'm frustrated because I cannot paint fast or fast enough! It is a good problem to have. This is also the quietest place ever. I want to remember so many things ... the old flesh-colored houses clothed with bright shutters and red geraniums, fields of golden sunflowers waiting to dawn, tall king and queen trees marching along the roadside, guiding us through to a view down an alley in a well-lit courtyard and then to a patchwork of orange rooftops and green fields.

The lights are about to go out in Villefranche. It is nearly 1 a.m. The market today in Montpon was wonderful, with so much happening. Life in France seems blissfully simple.

Simplicity is truly decadent. What clutter can you clear from your life to make way for more living?

Everyday Indulgence: Coq Au Vin

Ingredients

2 or 3 thick slices bacon, roughly chopped

1 organic chicken, cut into its pieces

Flour seasoned with salt and pepper, for dredging

1 pound button or cremini mushrooms (optional), rinsed and halved

6 carrots, peeled and sliced

2 cloves garlic, peeled and minced

2 large sweet onions, roughly chopped

1 bottle red or white wine

1 cup chicken stock

1 bay leaf

Bouquet garni of thyme, lavender and tarragon

Get all your ironing completed in the early afternoon. Move the ironing board out of the kitchen so you have more room, put on some frisky accordion music, and get to cooking. Over medium-high heat in a large pot, add your bacon and cook until it is crisp. It will stick at first until some of the fat is rendered, but do not fret. Once it is crisp, transfer to a plate out of the way.

Dredge your chicken pieces in the flour mixture, and then brown the meat in the rendered bacon fat. Put aside with the bacon. Now add the mushrooms, carrots, garlic and onions, and a bit of olive oil if the pan is too dry at this point. Sauté until they just begin to brown, which should take only about 5 minutes. Taste the wine, and if you like it pour half in the pot and cook for about 10 minutes to reduce it a bit. Add the chicken stock and the rest of the wine. Bring to a boil and add the chicken, bacon, bay leaf and bouquet garni. Return to a boil, then cover and simmer for an hour. Don't forget to remove the bay leaf and bouquet garni at the end. Enjoy dinner outside on the patio, even if you need your cardigan.

My Perfect Pairing: Domaine Pierre Damoy Chambertin-Clos de Bèze

From my notes: *Fresh laundry on the line at my grandmother's, geraniums in the sun, crushed walnuts and sugar cookies, M&M's, peonies, roller skates, raspberry pie, long silky finish*

Inspiration From My Notes: A Letter Never Sent

Dearest Judy,

The sea is angry now and I'm sitting on top of her. Guiseppe and I are at a tea room at dusk in a torre on the edge of the earth which is Amalfi. Below, the Mediterranean swings and pulls, licking her way up this cliff, almost reaching the great window we stare out of. It's the music of the sea and I am content to listen to her. The town is a bit below us and down the winding ribbon of road just a little way. We have been here for four days— eating fresh fruit with local red wine, buying bread each morning in the steamy shop where it's made. During the day we hide in our room or in quiet cafés from the tide of tourists who pour into Amalfi each morning. At night we go out—roaming the narrow whitewashed passages and staircases that connect secret places—out with the cats that moan and slink and beg for scraps at the back doors of trattorias. The lights of the small cliff-city shine at me now, like strange, low constellations, and the sea rolls on. I am in love and I may never come home. In two days we leave for the north, some days in Roma, forse (maybe) some in Venezia. I doubt we will stay in the nunnery (as you and I did so many years ago). I love you Judy. It's raining hard now. Amalfi is sliding down the window pane. But I can still see the water below. Be well.

When you become aware of the details around you, you are alive in the moment. If you take the time to write it down, you have the ability to revisit a special moment forever. What is happening right now with you that you would like to feel again someday? Photos save images, words preserve inner snapshots. Decadence is being able to look back with clarity and ahead with the wisdom it imparts.

Everyday Indulgence: Lemon Pasta

The silver Vespa wound its way impossibly in and out of the long line of nearly stopped traffic honking and smoking on the thin road we rode between Amalfi and Ravenna. To my left a cliff, to my right the sea 100 feet below with a wisp of a wall separating us from her.

A wiry Italian philosopher filled my arms and anchored me to the slippery scooter which he piloted deftly, weaving among the pushing bumpers and hulking tour buses threatening to knock us off the road. I closed my eyes when the calls came too close, held my breath and reinforced my hold on the hot Italian who sat between my thighs. We arrived in Ravenna in three whole pieces (counting the Vespa), with my adrenalin peaked in my veins. Along the way the peaceful scenery of the lemon trees, heavy with plump, sunny fruit and the promise of refreshment, helped to ease my nerves. And this is how I met Lemon Pasta.

Ingredients

1 good handful of spaghetti	Coarse salt
2 fresh organic lemons	White pepper
Olive oil	Fresh parsley
1 clove garlic, pressed	

The two of you return back home from a late summer bike ride around the vineyard. You shake out your ponytail and hop in the cool water of the shower while he makes a few refreshing gin and tonics. Open the windows wide and put on a pot of salted water while you are still in your damp towel. While it comes to a boil, throw on a dress or something. Damn gin's good. Grab a handful of parsley from your garden and savor the warm evening and the rest of your drink. Throw the pasta in the water and while it's cooking, scrub the lemons clean. Use a zester to scrape the lemon's peel, or trim the rind off of one lemon with a sharp knife and mince finely. When the pasta is done cooking, drain it well and set aside. In the pot you made the pasta in, add the pressed garlic and a few splashes of olive oil, salt and white pepper, heating through and browning just a touch. Add the pasta, the juice of 1 lemon and the zested or minced rind, and heat through. Taste it, and add more lemon and salt if you like. Serve with a generous sprinkling of parsley on top. What a perfect dish to restore you for the remainder of the night.

My Perfect Pairing: Cascina Val del Prete Luet Roero Arneis

From my notes: *Lavender, pear, sage, rosemary, light rose, honey tea and guava*

Inspiration From My Notes: 48-Hour Love Letter

I wanted to call but I did not call, because the spell that has been cast seems only to exist in the form of written word, a pure language instrument, a love-letter affair ...

I was born first of the five girls my mother would bear, which has granted me some character strengths and some flaws as well. (Am I older than you thought?) And I do need to know all about you—I want to poke around your soul with my pointy stick, gently lifting rocks and looking for jewel-colored bugs. Have I mentioned that I love bugs? I once sent a lover on a two-hour drive to retrieve my entire moth collection for an important art project; I was participating in a locked-in artists' retreat and we were not allowed to leave the building for 48 hours. Bless his heart, he did it. I still have the finished pieces. I named the collection Cowboy Dreams; it is centered on an old backgammon case painted white inside and is full of tiny little photos and gorgeous silver moths in various frozen positions.

Moths are my favorite: delicate, pale and mesmerized by the unique danger of candlelight.

My heart is beating in your palm.

For what would you lock yourself in for 48 hours? What is the one thing you could not live without? Why?

My Perfect Pairing: Château Latour 1961

From my notes: *Roses, cherry, unreal still, earth, Bourbon, cranberries, mushrooms, this wine is opening up like a paper flower in front of me; keep feeling like there is something ... now argyle, I feel like argyle ... is this fall time? Sweaters? Is that the tannin?—like licking an argyle sweater? Chocolate mint, dried grasses, Scotchy now. My, my, how complex you are*

Inspiration From My Notes: Greece Is Good
For Remembering

Today we went into town and visited Cara. She was making bread outside in her big ancient oven, which I love. Then here, to the beach at Mille, and swam far out, far enough to see Patricia's house, and it was so beautiful and afterward we took off our clothes and baked on the rocks and dreamed a bit. Now I am sitting here and I can feel the force of the water through the rocks beneath me. It is a strange, trembling sensation. The waves are big now and seem to be growing. I'm sitting in the very end of the sunlight and even as I write, the shadow of a mountain has slipped over this paper. The rocks all around are gray and red, covered with yellow flowers and green grass. The Mediterranean sings to me slowly and rhythmically, calling me back into her cold hands. I am mesmerized and relaxed under her spell.

Oddly, I'm thinking about home these days. Going back, being with family and friends. I am thinking of summer as though I have been hibernating. Thinking of warm days in the garden planting flowers, going to coffee early in the morning with good friends, barbeques and picnics on porches at night, riding in the car on sultry evenings in my thinnest T-shirt, going for ice cream and singing at the top of our lungs (I miss you Callie), listening to music and reading in the shady doorway. It is like I have been reborn and am seeing all these things there for the first time. I just want to go back and do it all again with my new eyes, and feel the deliciousness of regular, boring old life, in all of its mundane sublimity. Oh, the pull of days on end with nothing but work stretched ahead. Good old work and that solid feeling of accomplishment. I had become used to the idea of being a traveler for the rest of my life. Now I'm not so sure. Both options are equally enticing right now. It's the difference between the blue of the sky and the blue of the sea. Subtle. But you feel the intensity of each one just the same.

Sometimes you need to step back and make a little space to appreciate the decadence already present in your life. What do you do each day on autopilot? Are you missing something sublime right now?

Everyday Indulgence: Caramelized Onion And Trumpet Mushroom Pizza

I loved making this pizza when I lived at 239 East King Street. The owners of my little apartment had created a charming nest of a house (where they themselves had lived for almost 20 years). This place had many quirky, unique details added over the years to make their life in the small space more convenient. One of my favorite additions was the bread-rising rack that Mr. Fenner had specifically fashioned inside the cupboard just below the 1930s-era porcelain sink. This little nook also housed a miniature radiator, which provided the room with heat in winter. That ingenious little rack was perfect for bringing all sorts of yeast dough up to double in a wink. I still love making this pizza, in my new kitchen now, which I designed myself and which, of course, includes a sink that reminds me of my beloved old one back there on East King Street.

Dough

1 cup warm water

1 packet yeast

1 teaspoon honey

2 tablespoons olive oil, plus 1 teaspoon for oiling the dough bowl

Few pinches coarse salt

1 cup spelt flour

1 ½ cups white flour

Topping

2 large sweet onions, sliced

Coarse salt and freshly ground pepper

Olive oil

2 ounces Champagne or red wine, for deglazing

1 teaspoon sugar

12 ounces mushrooms, any combination (my favorites are cremini, Trumpet Royale, Alba Clamshell and Velvet Pioppini)

Mozzarella cheese, shredded

Parmesan cheese, shredded

Pizza may be the perfect food. So simple. The secret is a good crust. I love this one from my good friend Patricia. I like to make pizza when my friends come over as it is easy to prepare while visiting and there are lots of tasks to delegate while laughing the evening away and trying new wines. Of course you can vary the toppings, but this version is my ultimate go-to.

Preheat the oven to 250° F so that you have a warm place to set the dough to rise (if you do not have a handy bread-rising rack under your sink). Start the dough by first preparing a bowl, warming it under hot water. I find this helps kick start the yeast. Add the cup of warm water to the bowl, then the yeast, then the honey, whisking everything well for a minute. Once the mixture foams, place it near the oven and let it proof for about 10 minutes.

Once the yeast takes hold and bubbles start to form, add the olive oil and salt. Mix in the flour, ½ cup at a time, alternating the spelt flour and white flour until a smooth dough starts to form. It will take roughly 2 ½ cups total flour. (The spelt flour is a wonderful addition. It adds a nutty and slightly sweet dimension to the crust that is unique and delicious.) When the dough has formed, move it to a floured surface and knead it a few times to create a smooth ball. Place it in another warmed bowl, dried and rubbed with about a teaspoon of olive oil. Cover the dough bowl with a clean cloth, and set it in a warm place to rise. It needs about an hour to rise to double. Now you can go out back and saber that bottle of bubbles you have been chilling for your friends. What a party trick!

Back to business. In a large sauté pan, heat some olive oil seasoned with salt and pepper. Add the onions and the sugar, and cook over medium heat until caramelized. Salt as you go, so they sweat well and reach that mocha brown perfection. Deglaze the pan with half a glass of Champagne, or red if that is what is in yours, it will add even more dimension to the flavors. While the onions are cooking, sauté the mushrooms in a separate pan with a bit of salt. Keep them moving, but do let them take on color as they go. Once prepared, both onions and mushrooms can be set aside until the dough rises. (Of course, all can be prepared in advance, too, if you are entertaining and do not want to be at the stove.)

When the dough is ready, lightly punch it down, and let it rest for a moment while cranking the oven up to 450° F. Separate it into two balls for two separate pies. On a floured surface, press each ball into a flat round, transferring it to a foil-covered baking sheet when it is almost as thin as you want it, and finish flattening it there. Top each crust with olive oil and a sprinkling of salt, and par bake them for 10 minutes (less time if your crust is very thin). Once it turns just slightly golden, prick it with a fork to flatten the pillows, and add more olive oil, followed by onions, mushrooms, cheese and a bit more salt. Bake at 450° F for about 10 minutes, or until the cheese starts to turn golden brown.

This masterpiece won't make it to the table, so just slice it as it comes out of the oven, raise your glasses high in salute, and eat it standing around the kitchen. Why does everything taste better this way? Ah yes, it's the company.

My Perfect Pairing: Papapietro Perry Leras Family Vineyard

From my notes: *Hazel eyes and smarty pants, earthy softness, berry lip gloss, cherry love; the whole vineyard in my glass, making me a believer right there*

Inspiration From My Notes: Italy Is For Drivers

Notes from another trip to Italy, a gastronomic pilgrimage that took us across the north from Piedmont to the Italian Alps. Salute!

Remember running in the vineyards, Verduno, quiet streets, hot and dry, up at the park, kissing with lights below in the distance, warm nights. Tartare like red geranium blossoms piled on my plate, the first meal with the beautiful flowers against the dishes. Lovely wines, so many from so many regions! Barolo, Arneis, Barbera d'Asti, Lagrein! Valpolicella, more.

The full moon the second night at the castle and pulling pillows from the king's bed and making love on the floor in the moonlight for hours. The Johnnie Fabrizio lunch. My dramatic bra-fitting in Alba with the funny Italian woman who felt me up and then bent me over and taught me how to create cleavage the Italian way, by lifting each breast and plumping it in the cup; *"Stupende!"* she exclaimed as I stood up again.

The cheese trolley at the lake restaurant. Delicious stillness, the midnight walk in Sorisso. My solo run the next morning out into the countryside, Lago di Como, driving impossibly winding roads to forgotten churches full of mischievous angels. The manicured lawns and sparkling pools and perfect sunbathers, the vineyards and countryside on the road to Sondrio. The mountains! The unique and beautiful flavors at Siriola, flowers collected to be pressed forever in bound books, delicate as eyelashes on that overwhelming chunk of rocky Italian mountainside.

The meals! All of them! Breakfast and lunch, and accordion dancing with my new Nonna. The Castel dinner—more Castels! Del Pescatore and the moment I sat across from two men whom I love deeply, seeing them both with all of their idiosyncrasies, wonderful—what a pair! What a life!

Crying now remembering the courtyard at the Bergamo restaurant, my love looking at me, his eyes filled with tears, telling me moments later he felt that I was his mother and he was his father, the love that they felt for each other was like ours, him telling me that out in the beautiful hot night on the patio … so special, so simple, ciao Italia, una volta, ancora (once again).

Just when you think you missed the turn another roundabout appears. Make plans, allow for adventures. Less disappointment, more decadence.

Everyday Indulgence: Pork Belly With Cheese-Stuffed Medjool Dates

To purchase pork belly at my butcher I must order the entire underside of one pig. This means I usually have a freezer full of pork belly ready to go. What a decadent dish! I love it so and make it often as a treat for my friends and family. This version keeps the meat basic yet flavorful and is complemented by a sweet apricot chutney. When served with the dates, it is divine.

Ingredients

1 chunk pork belly, 1 to 2 pounds	Olive oil
1 large onion, cut in half	Coarse salt and white pepper

Chutney

2 tablespoons apricot jam (preferably one your mom sent you)	½ cup wine or sweet vermouth or some liqueur
Dried apricots	1 cinnamon stick
Dried figs	4 whole cloves
White raisins	¼ of a whole nutmeg, freshly grated

Dates

Goat cheese, softened

On a lazy day when you have nothing pressing in the afternoon, you may want to consider preparing this delicious dish. It takes awhile to make, though your hands-on time is nothing. Perfect for when you would like to slip in a little something else in the afternoon, preferably while the house becomes perfumed with one of the most decadent morsels available to mankind.

Preheat the oven to 325° F. Cut the onion in half and place flat sides down in a casserole dish. Add about a half-inch of water to the bottom of the pan. Score the fatty side of the pork with a very sharp knife, making slices every ¼ inch that reach almost to the meaty side but do not quite touch it. Rub the pork belly with just a bit of olive oil, then season it well with salt and white pepper, including inside the scored sections. Place the meat, scored, fat side up, on top of the onion, which will function as a sort of trivet, keeping the meat out of the water during the cooking. Roast the pork belly for 2 to 3 hours, checking that the water doesn't evaporate completely. The meat may curl; so pay attention that it doesn't slip off the onion and into the water during this phase. No basting is needed, just make sure you keep a bit of water in the bottom of the dish.

While the meat is cooking, make the apricot chutney. Add all the ingredients to a small saucepan. Bring to a boil, reduce heat, and simmer for at least 20 minutes. Turn off the heat and let the chutney's flavors marry while the meat continues to roast. Once the pork is done cooking, remove it from the oven and let it rest for 15 minutes or so.

Serve chunks of pork with the apricot chutney as a decadent starter or as a main course next to a salad and Patate Al Forno (see "Decadent Intercourses"). For the ultimate companion piece, simply slice the dates in half and stuff each half with a teaspoon or so of goat cheese.

My Perfect Pairing: Castello di Verduno Verduno Pelaverga Basadone

From my notes: *Grandma's house, waiting for breakfast, warm bacon fat and eggs with buttered toast. Light cedar, almost Pinot Noir profile in midpalate, lightest leather ever*

LUSCIOUS LIVING

Indeed there is opportunity for indulgence every day. Incorporate it in big or small doses, they both count. Decadence is as simple as a deep breath of fresh air, taken in with gratitude, grace and respect for the liberty with which our bodies do it for us all day long without our prompting. Shift your attention to the beauty around you and watch it settle on your smart hips like a divine petticoat—the dancing will likely follow.

Inspiration From My Notes: Mornings In The Bath

I love my bathtub. It's a vintage clawfoot, deep and perfect for soaking and one of the true simple joys in my life. We have all heard about the benefits of an evening soak before hitting the sheets, but baths are not just for nighttime—or weekends. Try this on a workday: Get up 20 or 30 minutes early. Run a bath and toss in some invigorating bath salts. Tie your hair up and make a great cup of coffee or tea while padding around in a thick robe and pretending you are at the spa. Indulge in your bath, and multi-task by reading the morning paper (do we still read those?) or checking e-mail while presoaking your stress away. BENEFIT: You will feel like you got away with something before anyone has even spoken to you AND you have already caught up on current events. Face the rest of your day with a serene "just back from the spa" smile and full-bodied, slightly wild beach hair (great for those who work at home such as myself, who may happen to have beach hair "at work" a lot anyway). Try this on your day off: Forget the paper and catch up on catalogs or that novel you have been saving. Have someone else make the coffee (unless you do it better) and serve it to you. Forget the timer and soak until you pucker.

Everyday Indulgence: Lamb Hash

This unexpected gem offers a substantial helping of decadence to start the day right. The first time I tried the dish which inspired this recipe followed a night of wild adventures involving a scandalous cadmium sunset over the hills of Sonoma, as well as her clear and most innocent sunrise.

Ingredients

1 whole leftover lamb shank	¾ cup Yukon gold potatoes, diced
Olive oil	Coarse salt and fresh pepper
¾ cup diced sweet red pepper	1 tablespoon fresh sage*
1 whole onion, diced	1 tablespoon rosemary*
¾ cup red-skin potatoes, diced	1 teaspoon caraway seeds

* *Is this in your garden?*

Pour yourself a cup of coffee or a pear sparkler. To make the sparkler, combine your favorite Champagne or sparkling wine with a splash of pear liqueur, in a pretty flute. Slip in a slice of fresh pear and enjoy. Kiss your mate, your pet or yourself and open the curtains. Do not get dressed.

Put a small covered pot of salted water on to boil for the potatoes. Sauté the onion in olive oil. Add the peppers and cook until they start to become tender. Add the potatoes to the boiling water. Shred the lamb, and add the meat to the onions and peppers. Season with salt, pepper, sage, rosemary and caraway to taste. When soft, add potatoes to the lamb and pepper mixture. Cover, and let the flavors marry for a bit while you make eggs the way you like (I prefer poached for this dish). If bread does not frighten you, toast away. Whatever blows your skirt up that day.

Serve with great coffee or another pear sparkler. If it is sunny, eat outside. If not, light a fire and snuggle nearby. You may never get dressed.

My Perfect Pairing: Billecart Salmon Blanc de Blancs Champagne

From my notes: *Grainy, green tea ice cream, soft and yeasty apple strudel with crunchy baked sugar on top, tastes like the feed store, yes! Going to Misch's market for Pop Rocks and sweet feed on a summer day*

Inspiration From My Notes: Come And Sit By My Fire

Another simple night in front of the fire. Sigh. I am so in love. I came home to this scene tonight.

The firelight flickered around, turning everything golden and warm in my living room, and where it couldn't reach, a candle had been placed. My love and I sat on a thick blanket on the floor, with all of the pillows from the sofas piled around us in a luxurious nest. He had made for me the most amazing cheese plate: There were so many cheeses—Morbier, aged Gouda, something very strong, and a truffled chèvre! Yum. Also, plenty of cured meats—somewhere he'd found salamis made of lamb and even wild boar. In the midst of these cheeses and meats, he'd piled a mound of almonds and drenched them in honey. This was our dinner, along with a bottle of bubbles. It was so fun, sitting there in front of the fire, having a picnic. I love listening to him and telling him all about my day. We lasted about an hour and a half before we jumped on each other. What that man gets me into is something else.

Why do we stop building tents in the house? A pile of pillows on the floor will make a fine foundation for your next indoor construction project. It's OK to stop there as long as you move in for a bit.

Everyday Indulgence: Fireside Picnics

I grew up as a little girl in snow country, and I have always loved the feeling of just tucking in for the night when the light faded early during the winter months. These days, when winter moves in to our Northern California home, and the rain blows sideways and the wind howls, I love to turn those early dark nights into a most romantic mini-getaway right in my living room. I light a bunch of candles, open a nice bottle of wine, move the coffee table out of the way and spread a thick, soft blanket in front of my hearth. No fireplace? No problem. Light a few more candles, and still make room on the floor to spread that blanket, like you would at the beach. Add throw pillows and you're set. Just leave room for a simple tray of delicious finger food. Make this a decadent snack event, but do try to keep everything simple so you can pile it all back onto one tray for quick clearing. You will find out why when you try this.

These picnics evoke a heavy dose of romance; so do not be surprised if you find yourself suddenly wearing only your socks. I like to also place a little, happy basket of sexy toys and playfully personal items within reach. Leave it peeking out a bit for your partner to see, and watch the reaction! This is a fun way to create intimacy with your mate, enjoy winter and try some decadent new foods (and positions).

I like to include sensuous finger food and anything considered an aphrodisiac. Think ultimate indulgence here: figs, chocolate, creamy cheeses, strawberries and raspberries, almonds and honey. If you are ambitious, oysters are a fine treat. Consider adding a whole vanilla bean to your glass of bubbles for a sexy twist on the pleasure of drinking sparkling wine.

Emergency version: You don't have the ingredients for a decadent snack tray but want to have a fireside picnic anyway? Grab your emergency bottle of bubbles (I keep several bottles of good yet affordable sparkling wine around the house at all times) and get off the couch! Do all of the above but don't worry about the food. In fact, you can even order something in if you're in serious need of restoration. I predict the rest will fall into place.

My Perfect Pairing: Château Latour 1959

From my notes: *Strawberry cheesecake, earthy, punky, fresh, delicious, and NEW; this wine is total youth and I remember the last time I could have had it, I am so glad to wait until now. Spice, structure, balance. Richness. Still long, long finish I can feel it in my mouth. Still in my mouth, still on my tongue*

Inspiration From My Notes: Taking Time Is Decadent

Back after a few days in the wine country of Oregon. It was beautiful there, with pretty fall leaves lighting the way, bright blue skies and cold! Nights wrapped in the arms of my lover, happy and warm. And tired now, too tired, but need to write more and get all of the revelations and feathery details down on paper for good. Just remember this …

We don't have long, do we? Each day is more precious than the last and they keep coming at me hurling themselves like leaves fluttering down from ash trees, whispering "water's near so come soon." I just want to stay awake and remember them all.

Taking time is decadent. Who do you need to call? Where do you need to visit?

Everyday Indulgence: Roast Duck With Wild Rice

I remember eating roast wild duck that my father had hunted. The flavor was good but the hazard was the very real possibility of cracking a molar on a wayward bit of buckshot. Dad always started those meals with that warning. Made it tough to relax. Not this duck.

Ingredients

4 organic oranges	1 whole clove
Fresh thyme	

Glaze

Juice from 3 whole oranges	1 whole clove
Juice from ½ lemon	2 tablespoons Grand Marnier
1 tablespoon honey	Coarse salt and fresh pepper
3 tablespoons Mama's homemade peach jam	1 whole star anise

1 box wild rice

1 pound mushrooms, diced into little boxes

1 whole duck, about 4 pounds

The most interesting thing to me about making a whole duck is the texture of the uncooked meat. There is something very sensual about the drape of the duck, the promise of succulence. Roasting a whole duck is a seductive task. When you are feeling particularly sexy, or if you would like to feel particularly sexy, I highly recommend it. Put on some music that speaks to your groin and begin by trimming the neck and wing tips from the duck.

Rest a roasting rack on top of a baking sheet. You want a place for the duck fat to fall, away from the meat. Now lay her on the lifted rack. Admire the way she drapes, velvety on top, ready to receive her seasoning of salt, pepper and herbs. Rub the inside of her cavity with salt and fresh thyme as well; isn't it interesting how that feels? Like wearing one doeskin glove for a second. Slice 1 whole orange and arrange the slices inside the duck, pricking a whole clove into the slice closest to the opening. This space is going to create a small well where the duck fat will collect in a slippery decadent pool during the roasting. The placement of that clove is not an accident. It will bask in the fat pool and release its essence into the rest of the meat while it cooks. Mmmmm. Inhale the scent of the fresh orange and thyme together, see how they play? With her breasts in the air, into the fire she goes at 350° F for the first hour and a half. Add a few tablespoons of water to the pan to keep the fat from smoking too much. Now, just leave her alone for a while.

You can create the glaze at this point. It is very simple. Add all of the ingredients in a small saucepan and bring them to a boil. Cook for a bit, then turn to very low and remove the star anise. It can overpower the sauce if you leave it in, but use your own judgment; perhaps you need some extra spice today? In any case, start glazing the duck after about the first 45 minutes of roasting. She will be spitting up a duck fat storm so if you are now wearing your bikini for whatever reason, put on an apron. (Yes, I cook in my bikini sometimes. But I like to call it my "office attire," as I often work on my patio actually, as after all everything is relative.).Baste the meat with the glaze, quenching her crisp skin perfectly.

Wild rice is a divine pleasure that starts with the first step, rinsing it. The black slender kernels give off the most unusual earthy tea scent when they become wet. Cover the rice with plenty of water, and bring to a boil. The rice will need about 45 minutes; cook it until you like the texture. I always add a fine dice of mushrooms, a whole pound of them, after sweating out their nectar in a wide saucepan on the side. All of these things are done easily, and slowly you feel a hush come over you and the sound of sizzling fat tugs at your hips and sends them swaying to set the table. How sexy was that? Who will you invite to dine with you on this beautiful night?

My Perfect Pairing: Evesham Wood Willamette Valley Pinot Noir

From my notes: *Chinese five-spice, horehound, love this dusty earth, roller skates on race day*

Inspiration From My Notes: The Small Notebook I Carry To Dinner

"I am packing for France and I am a sorry case. Book after book I need and it is so frustrating. One for writing, one for drawing, one for painting, one for writing another sort of thing, some for reading and on and on. It's awful, but I love them all and it simply can't be helped."

I wrote that journal entry years ago attempting to pack light in preparation for an extended European journey, some of which was intended to occur on foot. These days, I carry one small book wherever I go. Inside, I take tasting notes, make drawings, press flowers and leaves from memorable places, and store fortunes from crispy cookies. The quickly scribbled notes from these books, alongside my beloved journal collection, have helped to implement the book you are now holding. The point is, no matter how small and inconsequential your thoughts may seem in the moment, if you are moved to take note, that item is probably presenting itself for a reason to be revealed at a later date when you are really ready for the lesson. In our digital age, I have tried swapping my books for something more high tech. This may work for some, but I still need to touch the paper and feel the pen lay ink across it. I suppose it is the sensualist in me.

Go to a fancy stationary store or an art supply and pick out a beautiful little gem of a book. Make sure you like the texture of the paper and the way it feels in your hand while writing in it. Another consideration is will you be able to hold a glass of wine in the same hand and write notes at the same time? I have found some books to be helpful for this activity; others make it impossible. A small pen is a great idea as well, just tuck it inside the book. I like books with elastic wraps, snaps or ribbons that hold both the pen and book together while inside your handbag. Take the book to dinner and try to take tasting notes on whatever you try—food and wine. Write from the hip and open your mind. Think in many dimensions: aromas, flavors, temperatures and appearances. You will discover food all over again AND have a record of that wonderful new red you tried.

Everyday Indulgence: Meat-Stuffed Loaf With Mushrooms

There may be one burger in the world I place above all others. Not because of its towering height, but because of its sinfully layered construction, which includes a round of braised short ribs and a decadent heart of seared foie gras. I'm not giving up the game of finding a burger I like even more. But in the meantime, to calm my cravings I make this crazy thing.

Ingredients

1 full porterhouse steak (approximately 1 pound)

1 to 1 ½ pounds filet mignon

1 pound chanterelles or oyster mushrooms, sliced

1 tablespoon butter

3 leftover short ribs (about ¾ cup of shredded braised beef; see "Decadent Creation")

1 shallot, very finely diced

1 egg, whisked (I like to use a duck egg for this)

Coarse salt and fresh pepper

After a rainy spell and once the sun has come out for a few days, call that friend of yours, you know, the cute entomologist who likes to hunt for mushrooms in his spare time? See if he can score you a fresh batch in exchange for a decadent dinner. If you are the less-adventurous type, or don't have an actual mycologist in your little black book, pick up your own fungi at the local market and invite your accountant instead. In any case, you will need to begin this project by making the short ribs (see "Decadent Creation" for that recipe), either the day of or a few days in advance of your meatloaf date.

Once you have the short ribs worked out, this dish is quite simple. If possible, pre-chill the steaks in the freezer. About an hour will firm them up nicely and allow for easy slicing and pulsing in the food processor. Yes, you do need a bit of equipment for this recipe (sorry)! If that is not an option purchase high-quality ground meat; go for about 90% lean. Preheat the oven to 375° F. While it warms, prepare your custom-ground meat. Slice the steaks into 1-inch cubes, which is easier now because they're chilled. Save the bone from the porterhouse in your freezer for some soup later on. I do the meat in batches, and on the pulse setting as it produces a better texture. Pulse so that the meat is ground in nice small bits, not one big mushy glob. It is steak after all, and high end at that. You simply want it transformed into a delicate, tender state.

When all the meat is perfectly ground, put it in a bowl and re-chill in the refrigerator while you work on your mushrooms and your date, if he has arrived. Open some wine, or motion to him with your chin where the wine opener is (your hands are full of raw meat after all). Is he more ruggedly handsome than you remembered or is the candlelight working on you?

Ah ha! Time for the mushrooms. He has done well! They are so gorgeous and earthy. It's a big deal, let him know. If you in fact scored the mushrooms, show them off! How delicate they are with their feathery undersides and voluptuous tops and velvet crunch. (One of my secret pleasures is biting into raw mushrooms, especially firm varieties. It's a singular sensation, which always reminds me of softly nipping flesh, yum …)

Sweat the mushrooms over medium-high heat with nothing in the pan but salt. Yes, they will stick a little. Let them. Find your glass and talk to Entomologist/Accountant about his latest finds/field trips/acquisitions. Tell him about yours. Before you know it you will be jumping back to the pan, afraid something is on fire. That is a good time to add the butter. I like to include just a wee bit to richen up the mushrooms. Usually, they can stand alone. For this dish, they need a tiny bit of reinforcement and butter is the perfect ally. Melt it in, mix things up, turn off the heat and set aside.

To prepare the meat, mix into it one whisked egg (I like duck eggs, as I mentioned) salt and pepper and a very finely diced shallot. Yes, use your hands. It is very earthy and sensual. Entomologists (and accountants) love that stuff. Bottom line is, it works best and feels interesting. You can really connect with meat this way, trust me. You will *know* where things *are*.

In an 8-inch loaf pan (oiled, buttered or sprayed with cooking spray), press the meat into a shell of sorts, about ½-inch thick. Cover the bottom and sides, creating a little chamber for the filling, reserving about a quarter of the meat for the top of the loaf. Layer in the mushrooms, using about half of them. Next, nestle in the shredded short rib meat. On top of that, spread the rest of the mushrooms. Cover the whole thing with the remaining custom-ground meat, sealing all of the edges together so to be encased tightly in a perfect loaf.

Pop this in the oven to simply sear off the outside of the meatloaf. Remember, the short ribs and mushrooms are already cooked. The searing should occur in roughly 15 to 17 minutes. Keep an eye on it. If Entomologist/Accountant suggests trying another bottle at this point, I would go for it, but make him do the work while you watch what is happening in the oven. It is ready when indicated by a browned top and the same firmness test used for steak (it should feel like pushing into the flesh between your thumb and index finger if you like it on the pinker side). This dish is really easy to enjoy in front of the fire, on a plate on its own, with someone who likes bugs or numbers. Well, maybe just a little ketchup might be nice. Now, have you ever wondered why moths are so attracted to candlelight? Be careful. You could learn to like math tonight. Damn, these mushrooms *are good*.

My Perfect Pairing: Château Pradeaux Bandol

From my notes: *Great Geauga County Fair, sweet, sweat-heavy horse, caramel apple, dusty lane lined with apple trees and dried leaves, with plenty of muscle under that horsehide*

Inspiration From My Notes: Taking The Ride

What a day it was!

Up, and lots of work, and then a glorious horseback ride on the beach. The horses were new to me and they were spectacular: two Peruvian Paso Finos with the strangest, smoothest gaits in the world. I don't even know the names of the movements that they do, but they are unreal. My friend who owns them said that in Peru they have competitions where the rider holds a Champagne-filled flute and then goes through the paces—the rider with the most Champagne at the end wins, and often no one spills a drop! Champagne on horseback, imagine that! It is right up my alley, no?

One horse is bright copper and the other a rich espresso brown—both lovely and very sweet but a tiny bit wild still. I loved it. I ride with another woman who has two Arabians, the riding is very different—no Champagne! Her horses are for endurance riding, a type of marathon on horseback, very grueling and physical. The training rides that we do are tough. The horses runrunrun and I come home totally exhausted! Like the good tired feeling after a day of sledding in the snowy cold. But I still love it as well. The adrenaline is good. Next summer I may do a race with her; we will see.

Now the bath awaits. I hope the gypsy horses come and steal me in the night. They always take me on the best dream rides.

Ah, the luscious decadence of the end of a physically active day. What do you do that leaves you glowing, tired and deliciously content afterwards? Making love definitely counts. What ever it is, promise yourself to do it more.

Everyday Indulgence: Oysters With Champagne Wash

We once rented a house and spent several oddly sunny and sparkling summer days out at Bodega Bay, on the coast of California. On the way there, we stopped at Hog Island Oyster Company in Tomales Bay for a quick four-hour lunch. We bought 150 oysters on our way out the door. Suffice it to say, they are a powerful aphrodisiac. We didn't tire of their flavor or their spell for several magical days.

Ingredients

12 oysters, or at least 6 per person, any type you like (I encourage experimentation, but I love Kumamotos on the West Coast and Cushings on the East Coast).

Champagne Wash

½ cup seasoned rice wine vinegar

⅓ cup Champagne or sparkling wine

1 ½ tablespoons finely diced jalapeño pepper, seeds removed

1 tablespoon finely chopped cilantro

2 tablespoons finely sliced green onions

Big pinch salt

Mix up all ingredients for the wash first, and let the flavors marry while you shuck. On a bed of crushed ice, arrange the oysters on the half shell and serve immediately with the wash. Yum.

My Perfect Pairing: Henriot Brut

From my notes: *Entire bread shop, complete with pretty French girls riding bikes past the steamy windows, their fleshy, creamy, slightly sweaty thighs and wearing skirts in summer*

Inspiration From My Notes: Did Someone Say, Party?

What a beautiful night we had out at the party. Bring Your Own Magnum again proved that good things come in small packages *and big ones*. The wine! Some standouts from my notes: Heitz 2002 Martha's ... caramel, Coca Cola, sweet herbs. Another Heitz, Bella Oaks that was an entire pizza shop in a glass—creamy cheese, sausages, marinara, yes. We dove into a 1991 Hillside Shafer, and maybe there was a theme here at this wonderful Italian restaurant? Because my notes say: Spaghetti-O's (!) and still so bright and lively after all this time (really good). 2004 Carter To Kalon Cabernet spanked us with deep black cherry, earthy layers and was that an entire Havana cigar wrapped tight and sweet (or was Marvin there in spirit if not in person?). 2004 Harlan was rich and still incredibly tight "shameful to drink this so fast," I had written, but we knew even a magnum would be drained in a heartbeat at this party—even though we were almost first at the bar! Still, all the promises were there.

We had Coppola's Cask from 2005, a mouthful of Christmas cake, beautiful, a delightfully spiced nose. Also loved the '05 Scarecrow—a birthday party! Surprise wine of the night was the 2004 Aston Pinot— what softness ... "delicious, long finish on a whisper-soft Pinot Noir, delicate and subtle" were my exact words.

We had many more wines, but at a certain point in the night, a girl knows when to put down her pen and dance.

Can't wait 'til next year.

No, you cannot have too much decadence in your life.

Everyday indulgence: Rabbit Paparadelle

A late-summer Sunday is a good day to create this dish. The only thing I find difficult about it is quartering the rabbit. If possible, have your butcher do that.

Ingredients

1 rabbit, cut into pieces: legs, loins, ribs, back

Porcini mushroom salt, or dried porcinis and coarse salt

Flour, for dredging

Big bunch fresh sage, or 2 tablespoons dried, plus the same amount for "toasting" the meat later

8 sprigs fresh thyme

Olive oil

1 to 2 pats butter, plus 3 tablespoons for "toasting" meat later

1 carrot, diced

Two shallots, finely diced; ½ a medium onion also works fine

2 cups vegetable or chicken stock

2 cups (about half a bottle) Chardonnay or other dry white wine

Paparadelle

Dice. Dredge. Sear.
Dice in. Broth in. Wine in.
Oven 250. 2 hours.
Just kidding. Sort of.

"Summertime, and the livin' is easy…" plays like honey sliding off a hot spoon in the other room. You have a date with decadence, and he's waiting in your icebox. Rinse and dry the rabbit, then salt lightly with porcini salt. Dredge in flour, and salt the meat again while you heat your oil (a very generous coat of oil on the bottom of a Dutch oven will do it). Chop one-quarter of the bunch of sage, and crisp it in the oil, scenting it with the earthy herb. Watch the sage; if it starts to smoke, remove and discard, do not let it burn in the oil. You can add a bit of thyme and some salt to the oil as well. Sear the lightly floured meat on all sides, remove and set aside. Add the butter to the pan after the meat is all seared, and sauté the diced carrot and shallots a bit to season. Deglaze the pan with a few shakes of your wine just as the fat cooks out and the vegetables start to stick. This will loosen the flavors from the bottom and allow them to blend into the dish. Place the meat back in the pan, and draw a bath for the bunny of chicken stock and white wine. Coarsely chop most of the remaining sage, and

add to the pot with the thyme sprigs. Salt and pepper once more and braise for 2 hours at 250° F.

Rabbit is a delicate meat, our goal is to marry flavors and reduce the liquid. So go and relax under your plum tree and read a book or something for a while. It is Sunday, after all. If you are feeling more ambitious, now may be a good time to grate up all of those bricklike, aging odds and ends in your cheese drawer. My, how resourceful you are.

When the braising is complete, shut the oven off, and remove the meat from the braising liquid and allow it to cool. Cook the paparadelle to your liking in a salted boiling pot while you pull the rabbit meat from the bones. In a clean sauté pan, melt about 3 tablespoons butter, adding a bit of olive oil too if you like. Chop another nice bunch of sage, and crisp in the oil, salting and peppering a bit. Add the rabbit to your sauté pan and "toast" the shredded meat in the sage butter, crisping it slightly. Drain the pasta, and douse it with a bit of oil as well while it waits for the plate, tossing to coat. When the rabbit is nicely toasted, shut the heat off and toss the pasta into the sauté pan for just a moment to coat (not cook). Serve immediately, with or without grated cheese, and some fresh parsley if you have it. If the spirit moves you, dine under the plum tree on a comfortable blanket with the birds to keep you company. The leftover braising liquid is wonderful served with any remaining rabbit meat and simple buttery rice the next day. Add fresh peas and more carrots if you need to stretch it out a bit.

My Perfect Pairing: Traina Vineyards Cabernet Sauvignon

From my notes: *Spice, candied apple, cedar, warm vanilla wood smoke (still), bacon fat in back of the nose, unbelievably fresh and youthful! Beautiful balance, ripe cherry, tannins and acid both there and good, like a dusty porch at apple harvest*

Inspiration From My Notes: Fit For A Queen

I did not expect to see Oprah at this event, but there she was in all her sunny yellow glory. And she did sparkle like a light in all directions as she moved through the barrel room, which was stripped of its usual, tightly aging contents and filled with hundreds of auction barrels open and out for tasting. As Oprah and I tasted around the room, separately together, we found fun new selections from some of our favorite producers.

Barrels are tough—they can leave a lot to the imagination—but it's good practice to taste through them and fill in the layers where you think they will be later on in the bottle.

From my notes: I loved the D.R. Stephens '06 Cab—floral and jam with a soft nose. The Provenance was good as well, and Pride's buttered up Cabernet put a cookie in my nose and took me to another world. The polished Gemstone blend was a rich hit as well—with tasters and bidders alike.

It was the Mondavi To Kalon that knocked me out—and I don't think it was simply sentiment that made this wine tremendous, an '07 at that.

I barely got outside. Woodhouse Chocolate had a table full of love that I somehow couldn't tear myself from. And so I stayed, inside the cool, swirling my drop of Mondavi around like precious medicine in my glass, deciding on my next move, just a sip behind Oprah.

We all have a taste for decadence. What flavor is your favorite?

My Perfect Pairing: Robert Mondavi Cabernet Sauvignon Napa Valley Reserve 2004

From my notes: *Wonderfully balanced, delicious and deep, moving wine for Genevieve; pour your whole self into it*

DECADENCE OF LETTING GO

Too often I catch myself holding my breath. We train ourselves to work hard and push through each day as though the fate of the entire world is on our backs. We know the body becomes momentarily stronger when we hold an inhale, so that we may brace against what we feel is coming. If left unchecked over time the price of this kind of pressure can be steep. The result is a wound up, stressed out state of being that can become a bad habit or even a way of life. Let yourself let go.

Inspiration From My Notes: Mothers And Daughters

I just found a feather here in my journal book. I must have tucked it in between the pages some earlier day—I don't remember when. But it reminded me of a clear moment when I was about 16. Mom and I were out in the sunny pasture working on fences quietly together. One of my younger sisters arrived, upset over something with all of the passion a 5-year-old girl can conjure. Mom crouched down, in her jeans and work shirt, her dusty leather gloves off now, with my sister encircled in her arms. Suddenly my sister focused on something in Mom's plaid pocket—a bright blue feather. My sister stopped crying abruptly and reached to touch that soft and whimsical little feather. Mom said, "Oh hey, yeah, you like that? I've been saving that for you." My sister's teary eyes were now sparkling, at the feather. And that was that, problem solved. I knew Mom had probably slipped that pretty feather into her pocket when it caught her eye as we worked in the clear morning, of course with no idea at all that this scene waited.

It was such an incredible moment because it was then that I thought to myself, "So, that's what being a mom Is. Performance art. She's making it up as she goes along and she's brilliant." I was moved and remember it all in perfect detail even now 20 years later. And tonight here, I find my own feather. *"I've been saving that for you,"* my little book whispers. A message from the universe—taking care and inspiring me and pushing me in the right creative direction. Always.

Start collecting feathers, they are fantastic problem-solvers.

Most problems are not problems at all. Everything is relative. Pick one thing on your plate that is making you crazy and take two minutes to think about if it is really worth the stress it is generating. This kind of senseless worry simply robs us of our ability to let go and enjoy life. When you're done, delight in your commitment to release. Now go get coffee and celebrate your new freedom, which is also known as decadence.

Everyday Indulgence: Mama's Peach Pie

While my mom is more famous for teaching us how to flip off horses backwards and on purpose than for her cooking, when the woman makes pie watch out. She takes it seriously and it shows. Thanks Mama for your contribution. I promise to bring the ice cream and the bubbles.

This makes an 8- or 9-inch two-crust pie.

Pastry

2/3 cup plus 2 tablespoons shortening or lard (Gosh, really? OK Mom.)

2 cups all-purpose flour

1 teaspoon salt

4 to 5 tablespoons cold water

Peach Filling

1 cup sugar

1/4 cup all-purpose flour

1/4 teaspoon ground cinnamon

6 cups sliced fresh peaches (about 8 or 9 peaches)

1 teaspoon freshly squeezed lemon juice

2 tablespoons butter

To make the pastry, first clean up your freezer. You want your hands cold for this project; it is the secret to flaky crust. If your freezer is already clean, run your hands under very cold water for a minute. The pain is worth it. Using a medium-size mixing bowl (which you may also chill by putting it in the refrigerator for 20 minutes prior to making the crust), cut shortening into flour and salt until particles are the size of small peas. Sprinkle in COLD water, 1 tablespoon at a time, tossing with fork until all flour is moistened and pastry almost cleans the side of the bowl. Do not over-handle the pastry crust, as it will make it tough. Gather pastry into a ball with your very cold hands and divide into halves. Roll each one out on lightly floured board. Roll the pastry until it is 2 inches larger than an inverted pie plate using a lightly floured (and chilled) rolling pin.

Heat oven to 425° F.

To make the filling, you can heat your hands back up. Mix sugar, flour and cinnamon in a separate bowl. Stir in the peaches and lemon juice. Turn the juicy mixture into your pastry-lined pie plate. Dot the top of the pie filling with butter. Using parchment paper to transfer it (not your warm hands) drape the top crust over the filling. At our house you get points for creativity, so cut a pretty little design into the top of the pie to vent. You can use extra pieces of crust to make leaves or flowers as well and poke holes in curlicues like vines. Pretty! You need to chill your hands again so you can now seal the edges if you are a fluter. If you're a forker, just use a cold, floured fork. Mom is a fluter. Gram on the other hand was a forker who openly (and often) expressed her wish for Mom's knack with piecrust. I really think Gram's above-normal body temperature was the culprit for this small inability. Cover the edge with a 2- to 3-inch-wide strip of aluminum foil to prevent excessive browning; remove foil during the last 15 minutes of baking. Bake 35 to 45 minutes, until the crust is brown and juice begins to bubble through the slits in the crust. Serve warm by itself or with ice cream. ENJOY.

Love you,

Mom

My Perfect Pairing: Besserat de Bellefon Brut Rosé Champagne

From my notes: *This is Bouchon Bakery in a glass! Love this, root beer float with vanilla bean ice cream, like the quality of the caramelized, almost burnt crust on the top of Gramma's potica—wonderful depth and lightness combined*

Inspiration From My Notes: I Married Myself At 239 East King Street

Suddenly it is so clear what I need to do. And I feel so free! So free. Finally.

I don't have to make a decision about my entire life's fate today. I will go home and be by myself. I have much work to do. I will live alone in my apartment. I will make art there and song and music. My friends will visit me often and the walls will know their laughter again. And I will look for space somewhere. Space to have my art and nice windows for letting in light. I will be water, like a small ocean, and I will be soft and flowing and free and blue-green. I will look for a place where my horses can be. Where I can ride, where I can be whole. I do not want to be married. I do not want to be tied down to one place or person or idea. I will always remember to feel the fur of the wolf at my side. I will dig my fingers in deeply and feel how thick the fur is, how soft it is. How protective it is. It is all so clear. I feel so free. I have to make a drawing now. I can't write any more.

Decadence is inviting moments of calm clarity into your day. Step back and embrace the peace waiting for you in the space of your own self.

Everyday Indulgence: Beef Barley Soup

This is a very good soup to put together in a big batch, giving most away to friends who need it for whatever reason. It tastes best that way. My most memorable bowl was one shared with our friend Henry Hossfeld, one of our longtime grape suppliers. He had been battling illness for quite some time. We sat at his table with his wife and we all had the soup together. We were going to just drop it off, but Henry insisted we stay and enjoy it together, an impromptu lunch. Henry wore a quilt around his shoulders like a superhero's cape, and we all shared many stories and much laughter. Sadly, that was the last time I saw Henry; he passed shortly after that day.

We still get grapes from Henry's vineyard. His eldest daughter, Lucia, has picked up the labor of love her dad fought to build. Just like he blasted each hole for each vine years ago, she gets up each day and checks on them all. I think Henry walks the rows alongside her. That is what makes the wine so deep and full of character.

If you are fretting over a sick friend, know that cooking this soothing soup is as good for your soul as eating it is for theirs. Don't forget to include lots of well-wishing over the pot as it simmers.

Easy as pie this is. If you have any precooked short ribs on hand they are an excellent and tasty alternative to preparing fresh stew meat. If not, fresh meat works fine as well (see note *).

Ps. I recommend doing a big batch of short ribs when you make them for a dinner, leaving yourself with plenty of leftovers for options like this or Meat-Stuffed Loaf (see "Luscious Living"). Not to mention that they are damn good eaten plain and cold on their own right out of the icebox.

Ingredients

2 tablespoons olive oil

1 medium onion, coarsely chopped

2 shallots, minced

2 cloves garlic, minced

1 bunch carrots, peeled and sliced into wheels, ¼-inch thick

½ bunch celery, chopped

2 pounds cooked short ribs, with bones, or 1 ½ pounds stew meat, cut into ½-inch cubes and lightly dusted with salt, pepper and flour*

3 dashes Worcestershire sauce

1 bunch fresh sage, whole, or 1 ½ tablespoons dried sage

3 sprigs fresh thyme, or 1 teaspoon dried thyme

1 cup pearl barley

6 cups beef stock (made with 2 to 3 cubes beef bouillon and water)

*Note: If you use fresh stew meat instead of precooked short ribs, the only difference is to brown the meat along with the onions, shallots and garlic at the beginning. Once it's brown, toss everything in as outlined below.

Before you walk the dog, get this on the stove to simmer. (I know, he's giving you with "the look" but see if you can talk him into waiting just a little bit while you prep this.) I promise you will return to the scent of Heaven's Kitchen after you take your early evening jaunt with your best friend.

Heat the oil in a deep soup pot or Dutch oven. Add the onions, shallots and garlic, and cook briefly for just a bit of caramel color. Once you have that, add the rest of the ingredients. Yes, all of them. Throw the sage in whole, and swiftly zip the little leaves off the thyme with your fingers if you want to get fancy, discarding the stems. For the stock, heat the water separately in the microwave or on the stove, and whisk in the chopped beef bouillon cubes before adding to the pot.

Bring everything to a quick boil. This is a good time to add the well-wishing, get-better-soons and a few uplifting prayers or spells, depending on your situation. Once the pot boils, reduce the heat to a low simmer, top with a lid set at a slant to let the steam escape, and go for that walk. You both deserve it.

Admire the sunset and the orange leaves around your feet as you trot along. Red sky at night … see it won't really rain tomorrow! Well, if it does you have the perfect dinner on the menu. Either way, I promise that those on your gift list will appreciate the healing effect that this delicious, consoling concoction will bring. Consider adding ribbons and personal messages to the packages. You never know when you will see someone next. Life is like that. You might compose the messages while you are walking right now.

When you return home, check your creation. It will need a good hour and a half simmer in total. Adjust the seasonings to your liking, pull some of the beef from the bones if it is still hanging on, and incorporate it into the mix. Leave the bones in the pot all the way through; just let them do their magic here. You can skim the fat as it collects on the top of the soup, especially with short ribs there will be fat to remove.

When you can't stand it any longer, the soup is probably ready. Go ahead and dive in—you need to test it after all! Let it soothe your soul. Bask in the grounding quality of the barley. As you settle into the evening with the dog by your side, take stock of all that is simple and right in your world. Feel good about taking care of yourself. After all, it's the best way to prepare to take care of those around you. Good dog.

My Perfect Pairing: Carter Cellars Coliseum Block Cabernet Sauvignon

From my notes: *Deep, deep, deep as Henry's heart. I absolutely love this wine. Sumptuous balance. Red velvet wedding cake, candied jasmine and lush fruit glides over my happy tongue*

Inspiration From My Notes: Hot Springs Eternal, And Leaping From This To That

We opened the door of the low-slung villa and the coolness inside brushed a bit of the heat from us. It was dark. That first kiss up against the side of the car had taken years to manifest, and when it finally happened it held all the power of those days pent up like a thundering herd of pure red horses racing circles around my heart. It took us from the car to the mineral pool, and then against the wall under the tall trees, and now inside. He went to the kitchen to fix cocktails. I rummaged through the CD collection, left here for guests. It was an odd mix, from the typical (Pachelbel with Ocean Sounds) to the unexpected (Pat Benatar). I found the perfect middle ground, *Dino: The Essential Dean Martin*, and stuck it in the silver player, fast-forwarding to number five. Among the first notes of the song "Sway," my lover emerged from the kitchen with two gin and tonics, ice swirling in mismatched glasses. I walked over to him, the smooth, pale sienna tiles cool under my feet. We danced, touching only at the hips, his hands busy holding the cool glasses. And this is how the weekend at the villa began.

I took a cocktail from his hand and fished out one ice cube with my tongue, transferring it to his open lips as I kissed him. The living room merged into the bedroom, and after making love and soaking, inside the villa and out, I woke up sideways in the bed and it was tomorrow. I had no idea where I was, so I decided I must have died and gone to heaven. I was sure of it when an angel appeared in the doorway, vigorously swishing mouthwash from one cheek to the other, smiling the whole time. Not wanting to break my gaze or the spell, he swallowed it down in one gulp and exclaimed sweet good morning to me. The sun shined in on him and I could now plainly see his angel's wings for the first time: intricate layers of ivory feathers that glittered and sparked, like his electric green-gold eyes.

With everyone working herself to a pulp these days, and vacation time languishing due to fear of leaving work undone, we are a crazed society more inclined to rearrange our mobile phone apps than to gaze longingly into our mate's eyes over Mai Tais. While you may not have the time off, or the ability to get away for lengthy vacations, you most likely can sneak away for 72 hours (if you can't, you may want to look at why). From quaint and personal to anonymous and cavernous, you probably have many romantic getaway options for lodgings either in your own town or the town next door. Plan to leave on Friday night or Saturday morning. Since you are saving on travel, stay somewhere fabulous that you've always heard about at those chamber mixers your boss sends you to. Book a room with a fireplace and a fancy tub at the last minute and you may save even more. Just get out of your routine! Leave your laptop at home and hide your phone. Use all that time you would have spent on a long drive or plane ride and hold hands for awhile before dinner. On day two, slip in one more coffee (or maybe another two-hour lunch, food optional) and a stroll before you turn homeward. Return home in a flash, refreshed, reconnected and right around the corner. Try it.

Everyday Indulgence: Lamb Shanks Braised In Red Wine

The earthiness of this dish can be pointed in a few directions just by changing the vegetables that accompany it. As long as you begin with the holy trinity (onion, celery, carrots) you can vary the feeling with just a few adjustments. The following presentation makes use of the basics plus parsnips, which are lovely for late-winter lamb shank dinners. Spring might suggest pairing with freshly shelled snap peas. In fall, think about big warm chunks of sweet potato. Again, as long as you keep the holy trinity involved (amen!), feel free to experiment. Just don't mess with your foundation, that's what I always say.

Ingredients

2 organic, farm-raised lamb shanks (1 per person; if cooking for 4 or more, double the rest of the ingredients as needed)

Flour, for dredging

Coarse salt

Freshly ground pepper

½ teaspoon dried oregano

⅓ cup olive oil, for browning the meat

1 cup each chopped celery, carrots, onions, each divided into ½ cup portions

4 medium-size parsnips, peeled and quartered (think long and elegant)

2 cloves garlic, pressed

1 cup red wine (Syrah!)

1 cup beef stock, plus more for braising if necessary

½ teaspoons fresh thyme from your garden, or dried thyme

This is one of those recipes that is truly decadent on all levels. First, because it is delicious beyond your wildest dreams. Second, because it is so easy you will barely know you are cooking. Third, you assemble it and tuck it in the oven and are free to go and do something you love for an hour while it makes itself, which by my standards epitomizes decadence. Yes, *anything* you want. Permission granted! Go!

Rinse and gently pat dry your shanks like they just got out of the spa. Set aside. In a little side pot, put on some salted water to boil. In a bowl large enough for dredging, mix flour, salt and pepper, oregano (dried is better here so it blends with the other dry ingredients in the dredge). In a large skillet, heat the olive oil for searing the meat. Dredge the shanks in the seasoned flour, and brown them on all sides in the hot oil, including the flat ends. Place the browned meat in the bottom of your favorite baking dish that has a cover (I use a Dutch oven for this). Open the red wine and pour yourself a glass to make sure it isn't corked. Good? Good.

Now, add ½ cup each of the celery, carrots and onions plus the 2 pressed cloves of garlic and half of the parsnips to the hot oil. Over medium heat, brown the vegetables, then transfer them to the braising pot. Add the wine, beef stock, and fresh or dried thyme. Put the covered dish into a 350° F oven, and set the timer for an hour and a half.

Your side pot is boiling by now. Toss in the rest of the celery, carrots and onions, as well as the rest of the parsnips. This is the pretty set of vegetables. You are going to simply parboil them now, and drain. That's it. Go relax! Do what you like. Writhe all around in your decadent life!

Check the braise pot after about an hour for doneness. Keep an eye on it, and gently stir in your second set of vegetables. Mix everything a few times to baste. If the liquid is low, add more beef stock. Continue to cook the dish for another 20 to 30 minutes or until done.

A heavenly accompaniment to lamb shanks is the most simple salad ever: whole butterleaf lettuce (about 4 leaves per person) drizzled with cold walnut oil and sprinkled with coarse salt. I gently mix it in a big bowl to coat the leaves. No vinegar, no pepper. Do not mess with this preparation. It is absolutely refreshing with this voluptuous dish and will delight you with a nutty saltiness all its own. Pair it with the rest of the Syrah and have fun leaning back in your chair with satisfaction when you are done. Hey, good work.

My Perfect Pairing: T-Vine Napa Valley Calistoga Grenache

From my notes: *Lamb! Black raspberry red/black fruit, at the beginning pencil lead and now dusty Navajo blanket*

Inspiration From My Notes: Constellations

Suddenly I am quite calm and nicely balanced, and thought I best make a note of it. Part of it is my renewed faith in the afternoon cocktail. Part of it is just being able to let go and not worry so much. Part is my lessons learned in Italia. Those are: Take pleasure in what you have available to you. If that is the patch of afternoon sun on the patio—then that's it. Go for it. Take advantage. Use it. Do not think that something bigger and better waits in the wings. What you have available to you at most given moments is incredible if you would only stop and take notice of it. And so I am. And so it is.

Take tonight as an example. I am sitting outside on my patio, all alone, under strings of little lights, having a simple gin and tonic, eating good cheese and dried figs as this is all I have on hand. Seeing the constellations come into focus one after another, wrapped in fleece even¬ though there is no wind and certainly for the coast it's warm. And in the simplicity of this moment, I am very, very content.

Everyday Indulgence: Popcorn With Truffle Salt

I have taken up the slightly obnoxious habit of collecting salt. I mean, how different can they all taste, right? Amazingly different. Outrageously different. Obnoxiously different. I knew it was bad when I started wearing a locket filled with cypress flake, in case I found myself in a, well, pinch. (Sorry.) All that aside, truffle salt is something that could change your life forever.

I am a bit of a popcorn freak, which I blame on my father, who is addicted to it. Once when I was very young, he and I were whipping up a big stovetop batch of the stuff. While we waited for the oil to smoke, some wild prancing around the kitchen was started, and somehow I caught the handle of the saucepan in a horsey pirouette. Hot oil showered over me—I closed my eyes and ducked, and it landed in just one place that mattered. Although I had to endure the pain of the burn and the healing process, it left a beautiful, oval-shaped, pale-caramel-colored scar on my right arm just above the crook of my elbow. I always think of how much I love popcorn and my dad when I notice it. By the way, no movie required for popcorn. I have had many truffled popcorn and Champagne dinners. Thanks Pop.

There are no measurements for this one, just follow these instructions.

Coat the bottom of your favorite heavy-bottomed 1- or 2-quart saucepan with a film of olive oil during an early break in the movie you two are watching, and turn the heat beneath it to medium-high. Watch carefully for the oil to glisten, and refrain from large sweeping arm movements for a little bit. When it is very hot, add enough popcorn kernels to fill the bottom of the pan one kernel deep with no empty spaces. I find this is an odd and perfect ratio—the popcorn will pop and fill the pan exactly to the top if you do it this way. Reduce the heat to medium, and cover the pan with a tightly fitting lid. Let the pan sit still for a bit, maybe give it one shake every 10 seconds or so. No need to scramble it yet. As soon as you get a little action, however, you need to start your engine. I mix it up—back and forth, circles, cha cha cha. As the popping intensifies, you can play with the placement of the pan—I like to lift it up and off the heat to avoid any scorching, which is a major popcorn crime. For extra excitement, open the lid every now and then (if your dog will clean up the floor). You will know when you are done because the lid will lift off the pot and push into your hand a bit. After a snowstorm blessing of truffle salt is added, I love to eat this right out of the pan, as it remains warm for quite a while. No butter at my house, but if your decadence meter calls for it, I say add what you want just before the salt. Ah, heaven. Back to the flick.

Now, isn't that far more romantic than those bags that blow up in the microwave?

My Perfect Pairing: Domaine Etienne Sauzet Montrachet

From my notes: *Accordions and macaroons, paté (chilled), sugar donut (I got that after trying with an olive) and the overwhelming scent of old books at a quiet library, light almond, floral not sweet, soft, soft lilac on top of meringue. Thanks Cricket*

Inspiration From My Notes: Talk Dirty To Me (In The Car)

Oh my what a drive! The car was silver and fast and we had three hours to go. Suddenly his hand was on my thigh and after a thorough catching up on daily clients/problems/solutions, he said, "Hey, last night was pretty nice, huh?" and the conversation moved from there to what we both particularly liked about it. As the redwoods rushed by, I turned sideways in my seat to look him over, taking in the obvious shift in his lap. Talking about the prior experience had the same arousing effect as its actual happening. We often go along like this for some time, with the topic drifting from what we did and liked, to what we would like to do in the future. Nothing is off limits for us, which I love. This particular conversation got so steamy we finally had to, um, pull over for 20 minutes or so (I was not watching the time). It is amazing how limber and creative we really are.

This is a fun one. *If you have trouble talking freely about the indulgence of physical satisfaction and fantasies, the fact that you are driving may be just enough of a focus shift that it is no longer an issue. Don't you have somewhere to go? Like, now?*

Everyday Indulgence: Deviled Eggs

There is a running debate at our house on the process of preparing hard-boiled eggs. Does one use the cold water method or the hot water method? Cold water version says to add eggs to cold water, bring everything to a boil, shut off the heat and cover the eggs for about 20 minutes. The other method has one bring the water to a boil first, then add the eggs and boil for some time, then rest. Either way benefits from an ice water bath immediately following, which I'm convinced makes the eggshells easier to peel (not to be underestimated).

Ingredients

1 dozen organic eggs, hard-boiled, shells removed

2 tablespoons real mayonnaise

1 teaspoon Dijon mustard

Coarse salt

Ground white pepper

2 tablespoons sweet relish (optional), or sweet gherkins sliced into pinwheels

Paprika

Pull out your picnic basket and find your favorite sundress. Slice all of the eggs in half lengthwise, and scoop out the yellows into a small bowl. With a fork, blend them with the mayonnaise, mustard, salt and white pepper; add the relish if you like your devils on the sweeter side. Carefully press a spoonful of the mixture back into each egg-white "cup," or use a pastry bag and pipe the mix in for a fancier presentation. Whether you go rustic or uptown, dust them all with a cheerful sprinkling of paprika at the end. If you like, top each egg with gherkin pinwheels as well. The eggs should chill for a while in the refrigerator before you head to that picnic.

My Perfect Pairing: Château Rayas La Pialade Côtes du Rhône

From my notes: *Cigars, tobacco, earthy, foresty and hot like Polo cologne at the eighth grade dance in my cheerleader uniform with the panties attached*

Inspiration From My Notes: Storm Ponies On Sugarloaf Hill

I painted today and I'm feeling everything. A painting of the horses I saw in the rain from Saturday, the painting that I have had in my head since then, and it is truly beautiful. Tonight I think about so many things. Old things, ghosty things. And I am a bit drunk on rosé and cool evening time, and think of Amalfi and of Perugia.

This painting is not finished but soon will be and I love it so much. It is me—the horse—and all that pain around me is the rain and clouds and I stand with my broad back to it and endure, grounded, head down and serious, feeling the wet rain. Now, paint …

Later … finished finally, and happy with the work. It came out in a flow and I love it at the end with its swirls of energy and electric palette. The horses, they wanted to be ultramarine for some reason, and so they are.

Storms are part of life. It is how you navigate them that matters. Focus on the decadence of the satisfaction you will feel when the sky clears.

My Perfect Pairing: Oregon Black Walnut Liqueur

From my notes: *Hobnail boots at a barn dance on a cold December night, maybe November. Sulky racing ponies, pumpkin spice cake*

DECADENT CREATION

The creativity I have invited into my life fills my days and feeds my soul a good diet of sweet satisfaction. You owe it to yourself to tap into your imagination and release a few art babies into the universe. Do not be shy; go and find your outlet. What you make could carry on and inspire others, the ultimate gift of decadent creation.

Inspiration From My Notes: The Gypsy Ponies

Finding things again inside me like lost songs that I have loved and don't know why, just that I loved them—and this is a gift to myself for goodness and truth and light—and the journey carries on and transforms me through sound and sight. I love this life!

Having begun the "gypsy ponies," my new painting series, I love them deeply already. Began with a large piece just because the big canvas was ready. The first is called "from this to that." It is very dramatic—two horses leaping through the air—boldly, wildly, beautifully. Listened to Amélie's music and Sigur Rós all day; they were just the right influence and vibration. Very lovely.

An airplane crosses my studio sky, red lights pulsing in time to the music now Sigur #3, and my own heavy horse is reflected there above, the plane a heartbeat over me, so amazing. It all feels like a giving away of myself that bounces back, and the more it does the more I want to give—perfect soul food, painting is.

The act of creating can be as simple as releasing your thoughts about one little thing in your private journal, or cooking a luscious meal, or as elaborate as making a thousand paper cranes and stringing them together with deep purple thread. The path is the same: To get there, you must open yourself and touch the source of your own creation space. It's a ride worth taking. You never know what lies along the path of discovery. It is almost always more than you thought you would find.

Everyday Indulgence: Pork Loin With Lavender, Figs and Filberts

If there is one perfect fruit in this world, for me it is the humble fig. Offering such simple and sensual flavor. Oh, how I love them. They have always reminded me of the origin of Creation with their ambiguously sexy package. No need to go squeezing every one at the shop to test for that giving ripeness. Select figs that are weeping a drop of nectar at their base, they will be sweet and succulent. This is a delicious way to use them when in seasonal abundance.

Ingredients

Fine pork loin

1½ cups filberts, chopped between coarse and fine

20 plump figs, any type, the sweeter the better

¼ cup turbinado sugar, or 3 tablespoons honey

Olive oil

Coarse salt and fresh pepper

Large bunch fresh lavender, or about 1 cup dried lavender

Light some candles, pin up your hair and pinch your cheeks pink. Put a bottle of Sauvignon Blanc in the fridge to chill.

Prepare the pork by cutting the loin in half (*not lengthwise!*) if it's long. Using a long skinny object, make a tunnel in the center of the meat. I use my knife-sharpener tool, first scoring the end of the loin, then working in the sharpener and slowly opening a tunnel all the way through. You will be stuffing this cavity, so make it decent capacity. Chop the filberts and the figs, and right there on the cutting board, add sugar or honey and work them together into a thick, gooey filling. Sprinkle the filling with salt and pepper while you work. Once it's really mixed together well, stuff the mixture into the tunnel you created in the loin. (It will seem strange at first. Keep going.)

Remove the Sauvignon Blanc from the fridge and pour yourself a glass. Appreciate its scent and flavor now, before you start working with the lavender. If you have it, grab a big handful from your garden. Remove the flowers from the stalks and lightly squeeze them with your hands to slightly release their oil, discarding the stalks. The kitchen is going to smell like a medicine shop at this point, but do not worry! Rub the stuffed loin with oil, salt and pepper, and then carefully roll it in the lavender. It does not need to be completely covered.

In a large pan ready with hot oil, add the seasoned loin and sear the meat. You will lose some of the lavender here; don't fret. Move the seared loin into a foil-lined broiler pan or tray, and broil the meat for about 9 minutes on each side. The lavender will crisp up; you actually want it crunchy, well done and smoky. This will caramelize the lavender, changing it from a perfumed coating into a divinely delicate and totally unique flavoring for the meat.

When the loin is cooked to taste, remove it and let it rest. Turn on the fan or open the back door, letting the smoke out of the kitchen. Take your glass of wine and go enjoy the sunset for a moment while the air clears.

Serve this dish with a simple salad and wild rice with butter and salt. If you prefer to move to red wine, Grenache is a lovely natural.

My Perfect Pairing: Sin Que Non The Naked Truth Estate Grenache

From my notes: *Honey bee–stung berries, berries! Love this wine, color so dark! So balanced and luscious, it's all good angel/bad angel, like a cool ride on a fast motorcycle on a hot June day, ripe (tasted in magnum)*

From My Notes: My First-Born Child Was A Rhône Blend Named The Archer

As an artist, creation has always been an inextricable part of me. There has never been a time in my life that was not spent making something. Art balances me, and gives my energy a positive channel through which to flow out into the world. My high-set hope has always been that my paintings and drawings would go on to inspire others and bring joy into their lives. But I realize that visual art has some limitations. Only those who stumble upon it will get to feel its impact. Depending on where and how the work is shown or reproduced (or not), this can only expose the art to a handful of people, relatively speaking.

What has always amazed me most about wine is its ability to reach and touch large and wildly diverse audiences, in even the most distant locations, the most unlikely circumstances. I've often thought how incredible it must be to create something with passion that goes out into the world and becomes so intimate a part of the lives of others. What a wonderful sensation a winemaker must feel when he or she produces something that will go on to touch the lives of so many people in ways too many to count! The bottle opened at the dinner party for the friend who just finished a doctorate. The wine selected for the toast between lovers who have decided to wed. The glasses passed among a family mourning the loss of someone close. The cork popped on the gorgeous snowed-in night that inspired a fireside picnic that led to the mad lovemaking that gave you your precious baby girl with the wavy hair and your wife's sweet cheekbones and fine jaw. The power of wine, subtle yet profound, is what has always made me ache with admiration for those who dedicate their lives to its creation and perfection.

That is why, though an amateur, I decided to produce my own wine. I saw it as creating my most layered, multidimensional piece of art to date—one that people were going to ingest. From the flavors of each element of the blend, to the artwork on the packaging itself, it was the single most stressful and sublime creative project of my life thus far. With no kids of my own, I have to say that for me it will be the closest I get to being a new mother. The anticipation of aging, the delighted surprise in meeting the package the first time it is carefully placed into your exhausted arms. If a new mother could pick out her offspring in a dark room on smell alone, well, so could I.

What is your big dream-goal? Does it feel far away? Think about the steps it might take to get where you want to be and write them down. Can you do a step today? Do it. Can you do another tomorrow? A little attention each day spent on something that you feel passionate about can lead to big things. Decadence is caring for yourself and cultivating a positive mindset about reaching new heights.

Everyday Indulgence: Braised Short Ribs With Rustic Mashed Potatoes

While this dish is robust enough to hang on a hunting trip with the boys, I like to make it for a night in with a girlfriend or two. When you have a packed day and hit the ground running, consider making short ribs. They take only a bit of time to prepare, and they do incredible things in the oven on their own. You can wait until the end of the cooking time to do the potatoes. That will give you more time for chatting.

Ingredients

3 pounds bone-in beef short ribs

1/4 pound pork belly or bacon, coarsely chopped

Lavender salt

Flour, for dredging

1 medium onion, diced

2 carrots, peeled and diced

1 firm apple, peeled and diced (I like Gravenstein)

1 firm pear, peeled and diced (I like Bartlett)

Coarse salt and fresh pepper

8 leaves fresh sage

2 sprigs fresh rosemary

Red wine (I like a nice Syrah for this)

2 ½ cups beef stock

Rustic Potatoes

1 pound Yukon Gold fingerling potatoes

Sprig rosemary

Coarse salt and fresh pepper

Dash olive oil

2 tablespoons milk

2 tablespoons water or chicken stock

Connect with your best girlfriend and have her plan to pick up some bubbles on her way to your house at five. You are going to use your lunch hour to get this baby in the oven, which is great if you work at home like I do and work happens to be one flight of stairs away from the kitchen.

Preheat the oven to 350° F. Prep your onion, carrots, apple and pear into a nice, neat dice and set aside in a pretty pile. Brown the pork belly (or bacon) in a heavy Dutch oven, crisping it over medium-high heat to render the fat. I like to add coarse lavender salt to the pork belly, quite a bit actually, as pork belly is not salty at all and likes the flavor (use less if you are preparing this with bacon). Watch for spitting! Pork belly is a well-known spitter when done on top of the stove. Once the pork is crispy, remove it from the fat and set it aside.

Salt and pepper the short ribs well (you can use more lavender salt here in addition to regular coarse salt), trimming off any thick outer skin if necessary. I like to get rid of the tough stuff. Dredge the ribs lightly in flour, season a bit more with salt and pepper, and brown the meat quickly in the rendered pork fat. Add in a few sage leaves. Make sure to sear all sides of the meat. While you are waiting for the meat to brown this way, open a bottle of red wine, and set aside (or test it if you feel the urge and your afternoon is lighter than your morning was!). Ready your beef stock.

Once the rib meat is seared, move it off to the side for a moment. Add all the prepped dice to the hot fat, and cook for a bit so everything begins to soften slightly. Once it has, add half the bottle of wine, and bring to a bubbly boil. Cook it for just a bit, then add the beef stock. Give it all a good stir, and then nestle in the short ribs. They should be mostly submerged in liquid, so adjust the level of stock if necessary. Chop the remaining herbs and add them in, along with more salt and pepper to taste. Check your watch; add a lid and place the pot in the oven at 350° F for about 2 hours. On your afternoon break, turn the oven down to about 325° F, and if there's a lot of liquid in the pot, leave the lid off for the remainder of the cooking time to thicken the whole braise up. If you do not work at home, this might be a good afternoon to develop a case of "girl trouble" (then you can go and find yourself some). Otherwise, check out of work early and finish your project.

The potatoes? Easy. Best done while brandishing a Champagne flute in one hand and talking to your girlfriend with the other. (Who by this time has appeared on your steps with a bottle that goes POP.) Prepare a small pot of salted water and bring to boil while you coarsely chop the fingerlings (no peeling necessary) to the sounds of *"Can you believe he did that!"* Boil the potatoes for about 5 minutes (they are babies, after all) then drain. *"NO, I CANNOT,"* you tell her in disbelief while leaning over the hot water as you pour it out for an impromptu steamy facial. Put the pan back on the stove; you will use it again.

"I know," she says, rolling her eyes, while you place the potatoes on a baking sheet and toss them with a splash of olive oil, flick of salt, twist of pepper and any remaining herbs. Now into the oven they go for a bit of roasting and more flavor. You'll have to slide them onto another rack if the ribs are still giving up the ghost in there. *"Well are you surprised? I'm not. I just can't believe he did it where he did!"* And you both double over, laughing. Roast the golden potatoes for about 15 minutes, or just until they start to go brown. When they do, pull them out, put them back into the pan you started with on the stove, and add the milk (a couple small chugs from the carton is usually about 2 tablespoons). If you have butter, add a couple pats, or use a few splashes of olive oil.

With a fork, smash the potatoes into a crude pile, then add the chicken stock a tablespoon at a time as you stir to perfection. Season to taste, taste as you go, and stop when you're happy. Do no get so caught up in catching up that you overstir the potatoes, as they can get gluey quickly. This skin-on version has great texture and extra nutrients, too, and goes great with the short ribs, which are either already out or coming out now. Plate them with the luscious potatoes and sit yourselves down. *"Now, where did you say you met him?"*

My Perfect Pairing: Ruby Kurant The Archer

From my notes: *Butter cookies, blackberry jam, rich and spicy layered on top of earth and crispy salmon skin, cacao nibs, yes, that is dark chocolate!*

Inspiration From My Notes: Van Gogh, A Love Affair

I spent some time in the Netherlands during my studies. There, without peers my own age, I passed my days soaking up contemporary art, which turned out to be quite dangerous. Following are just some of my impressions, pulled right from my sketchbooks.

Van Gogh the beginning ... even his studies from plaster statuettes were unbelievable ... then he adds to them color, and they breathe ....

This is almost too much for me to bear. Until today I have only read about these paintings and now they are so alive in front of me I am almost crying seeing them—knowing what pain Vincent must have felt. It is almost too much. Oh, now I am losing control! I have come to the Japanese prints and the blossoms the blossoms are so delicate and insanely thick I can smell them, and suddenly Kerouac is here with me as well and all the bodhisattvas, all of them. This touches me so deeply ... the flowering plum tree ... oh my ... red orange pale white yellow brown black plum.

Yet more discoveries on this day in November here in the Van Gogh museum. Looking at the painting of Wheat Field with a Lark, it's not so much love of art that I feel but rather love of nature. And I'm hearing the wind across that grass and it sounds beautiful and you see all of those skies and clouds and fields all in his eyes and they ARE there—the reflection of chaotic light in branches and in leaves.

I have lost track of my time here, in Vincent's place again seeing the tins and the letter folders that Johanna used to keep his words, and I wonder how many times her fingers tied the ribbons together around that strange correspondence. There are so many people here today. Why don't I feel good about that? Do I want to keep him all to myself? Maybe to protect him from those who do not understand him. Standing in front of the church at Nuenen and feeling the cold of the February days—and I am at Gramma's house outside in the bare branch yard on frozen, muddy ground, thin yellow light of day, laughing and playing with my younger sister.

Museum revelations and observations; watching people today. A boy so attached to his lover she had to pull away from under his weight. A young girl on tall legs with a short white sweater and bobbed strawberry blond hair. So many people, so many people ... watching Vincent, watching them.

Art reminds us to pay attention the details. You can't create decadence if you don't notice it.

My Perfect Pairing: Patricia Green Cellars Pinot Noir Croft Vineyard

From my notes: *Amazing nose, with creamy cheese, hide, sweet marjoram; absolutely lush, smooth, balanced fruit, like some kind of cosmic Pop-Tart covered with dark chocolate*

Inspiration From My Notes: The Lost Decadence Of Abundant Accomplishment

In an act of dedication to my art and producing it, I did not own a television for 10 consecutive years. That time in my life was marked by a blissful sense of peace and quiet full of uninterrupted blocks of time to create, and also by my total lack of knowledge of current affairs. I'm hoping it was a slow decade. (How would I know?) Life without TV taught me how little I needed it, and what price I'd paid to include it in my day. Which happened to be, a lot of time and mental energy worrying about an endless list of products and people that I had absolutely no control over nor interest in, but that suddenly became the intimate focus of my own thoughts and worry. During my TV-less time, I created countless paintings, drawings, sculptures, gardens, silkscreen T-shirts, bumper stickers, relationships and dreams while filling a dozen and a half journals with words. A good decade's worth of work.

If you can, try a little less TV in your day. Walk your dog again. Talk to your neighbor. Knit. Hide the remote and say you think you took it out with the recycling. See how long you (both) can stand it.

Everyday Indulgence: Cassoulet

This is the kind of decadence that takes a bit of planning and a fair amount of commitment. I have settled on a slightly simplified version here, foregoing a few of the items that some classic recipes insist upon. It's an absolute meat feast—I use duck, lamb, kielbasa, bacon and pork shoulder, but feel free to mix and match and substitute meats that you like or can easily obtain. It takes awhile and makes quite a mess, at least the way I cook, but it's worth it. Share it with a few friends, as it yields a whole lot of deliciousness.

Ingredients

1 2-pound duck (or a small chicken), gizzards reserved

1 2-pound pork shoulder or pork butt

2 lamb shanks

1 pound bacon

1 pound kielbasa

Coarse salt and fresh pepper

Olive oil

3 cans Great Northern beans

2 cans white kidney beans

½ teaspoon cinnamon

½ teaspoon pumpkin pie spice, or allspice

¼ teaspoon ground nutmeg

1 teaspoon dry thyme

1 large onion, chopped (about 2 cups)

6 cloves garlic

3 large carrots, sliced (about 2 cups)

2 cups dry vermouth

1 tablespoon fresh rosemary or 1½ tablespoons dried rosemary

5 cups beef broth, using 2 bouillon cubes

6-ounce can tomato paste

2 teaspoons fresh thyme

Bay leaf

Crumb Topping

4 cups bread crumbs

¾ cup chopped fresh parsley

Check the weather report. If you see a day of sun followed by several days of rain, it is a good time to make yourself a little cassoulet. Use the day of sunshine to shop at your favorite market. Have a coffee with your friends on a sunny sidewalk and invite them to dinner tomorrow. When you awake and can hear the first raindrops on your roof, it is time to make the cassoulet.

Preheat the oven to 450° F. Rinse the duck, pork shoulder and lamb shanks in cold water, pat dry, and season with salt and pepper. Cube the pork shoulder into 1-inch pieces and set aside. Place the duck breast up on a rack set on top of a baking sheet (the higher the sides, the better). On a second rack on a separate baking sheet, put the two lamb shanks side by side. Slide both shanks and duck into the oven. Roast at 450° F for 45 minutes.

Meanwhile, empty all 5 cans of beans into a large Dutch oven and set aside for now.

In another skillet, brown the pork shoulder cubes, adding the gizzards plus the cinnamon, pumpkin pie spice, nutmeg and the teaspoon of dry thyme. Brown the meat, adding a little oil if it sticks to the pan. Once the pork has a bit of a head start, add half of the bacon, the onion, half the garlic (about 3 cloves) and all of the carrots. Continue turning the mix until the vegetables are cooked through. In another skillet, fry the rest of the bacon on its own until crisp. Check your lamb shanks now, they may need turning; if the meat is pulling away from the bone, that is a good indicator.

Once the pork and vegetables are ready (brown meat, par-cooked vegetables), remove them from the fire and add on top of your beans in the big pot, but do not add the liquid from the pork pan, rather, if it is excessive, drain most of it away, and don't clean the pan as you will now deglaze it with 2 cups of dry vermouth. From the bacon skillet, move the crisp pieces to the big pot, reserving the rendered fat; just set that skillet aside, no deglazing here. Check the duck, it should be sizzling now, and raining silky fat into the dripping pan below it. Ah yes.

After deglazing, use the big skillet to cook the kielbasa. Add a bit of water, and cook for 20 minutes or so. Slice the sausages and add them to the big pot.

Next, make 5 cups of beef broth in this same skillet. (Why dirty another pan? Do you have any left by now, anyway?) While it simmers gently over very low heat, just enough to get it to emulsify, add the tomato paste and gently mix it in. While that is marrying, pull the shanks from the oven and set aside for a bit of a cool down. The duck should be ready now as well, so shut the oven off and let her rest in there. Now, pour the beef and tomato liquid into the large pot, on top of everything. When you can handle the lamb shanks, cut away most of the meat from the bone and place it in the pot, followed by the shank bones themselves.

This is a good time to split the cassoulet into two pans, if you are out of room. Quarter the duck and place half in each pan. Move one shank bone to the second pan, and split the rest of the mixture up as well. Now, add the rest of the garlic, the rosemary, the fresh thyme, a bay leaf (add a bay leaf to each pot if you have two, and divide up the herbs as best you can).

Cover the pot(s) and place in the oven at 350° F for about an hour. Check the liquid levels: if too wet, continue cooking uncovered; if dry, leave the lid(s) on (or add more beef broth).

Stand back and take a deep breath before attacking the mess in your kitchen. Promise yourself a glass of Champagne as soon as the pots are scrubbed and the duck fat is sopped off the counter tops.

That task behind you, go ahead, pop a cork and indulge. Good grief, no one deserves it more than you. Turn the oven down to 325° F at this point (I am assuming it took an hour to clean the kitchen). You can also nudge the meat back down below the surface if you like. Turn the oven off for a rest after about an hour and a half total cooking time.

For the crumb topping, combine 4 cups breadcrumbs (I like the prepared version for this since everything else is so labor intensive) with ¾ cup chopped fresh parsley. Sprinkle half the crumb mix on top of the cassoulet, and bake uncovered for about 45 minutes at 450° F. This is a great time to take a bath and have a second glass of bubbles. Then you need to hop out and get serious again. Stir the first batch of crumb topping into the cassoulet. Sprinkle the remaining crumb mix on the top, and bake for another 30 to 45 minutes at 450° F. Get dressed, light a fire, dim the lights, set the table and welcome your guests, they're at your front door now. Don't be surprised if they have found your house on scent alone.

My Perfect Pairing: Antinori Cabernet Sauvignon Antica

From my notes: *Cabernet! O my! Anise, dust, gorgeous nose, pelt, fur, cashmere berries, yes! "Put that in your book …"*

Inspiration From My Notes: How To Host A Blind Tasting

For years, I was a regular with a blind-tasting group, comprising mostly men, that met on Monday nights. An eclectic collection of wine lovers, we gathered religiously to grill meat, watch football, drink blind and rowdily debate vineyards, vintages, winemakers and labels. Not a traditional blind tasting, but educational all the same. I took copious notes, scribbled in crazy penmanship in black books, and always brought my full collection of past notes for cross-referencing. I slowly gained a flavor and scent library of my own while asking questions and trying to ignore the game on TV behind me, which was incongruent but unavoidable. While it wasn't a pure tasting environment by any stretch of the imagination (many of my wine notes refer to smoky qualities probably imparted more from the roasting meat on the grill just outside the screen door than from any character the wine was offering on its own), I learned a ton about wine just from trying so many and analyzing them so closely. Correct answers, even in varietal only, were highly regarded and I became passionate about upping my average.

The table was always covered with half-filled carafes intentionally void of description save the pet names we gave them—the beaker, the saucer, the kiss—so we'd have a reference point when we all passed the same wine around and the guessing game began. This I loved the most, and as we all tasted and talked and swirled and tasted more, the familiar "hold it, hold it, hold it!" of one of the regular members would surely ring out just as the owner of that wine was about to make his big reveal. The only question we were allowed to ask while making our determinations: "What time was this wine opened?" I adored this game. I think the group was at least entertained by my passion and obscure observations. I am thankful now that I have books full of notes from these fantastic nights complete with sketches of the carafes next to my strange descriptors. "This wine tastes like a wedding dress!" I exclaimed one night to a room of blank stares. Finally someone said, "Before or after the wedding?"

If you want to host a more serious blind tasting event, you will want to avoid serving much more than some basic pearly crackers and water on the side. Save the meal for afterward. Let folks know to forego heavy perfumes or scented body products that would interfere with the delicate task of dissecting the aromas in a glass of wine. Have a wine wheel around, just for fun. If you are feeling very ambitious, you may want to include some small covered bowls filled with a variety of classic scents one might find in wine (i.e., fresh blackberries, dried figs, apricots, honey, sliced cherries, rose petals, jasmine, etc.), which will help guests orient themselves to these aromas. It is great for olfactory training and makes it easier to identify the scent in the glass. Provide water to keep everyone hydrated, and a dump bucket where guests can pour out leftover wine to move onto the next one. Put out some simple white crackers as a palate cleanser between wines if you plan to pour a diverse line up. Provide paper and pencils for note taking. Last rule, use good stemware! You do not have to break the bank on expensive varietal versions, but at least provide adequately sized glasses for reds and flutes for sparkling wines.

If you take just these few things into consideration you will be set up to get the most out of the tasting. From there, relax and have fun. Instruct guests to bring bottles already decanted, with the bottle and cork sealed in a brown bag. You can choose to have a theme such as a varietal, a region, a country or even a producer. It can be all white, all red, all sparkling, or a mix. There are no rules. It is all about education. Pour a small sample in everyone's glass, try the wine, then go around the room allowing each person to talk about the wine and make their guesses as to what it is—usually starting with the varietal and going into more detail from there. Reveal the wine only after each person has had a chance to participate. Encourage discussion, don't take it too seriously and have fun. After all, it's only wine.

Everyday Indulgence: Roasted Potato Slices With Brie And Avocado

This is my version of a delicacy we shared on those Monday nights. Somehow the little morsels paired perfectly week after week with many of the wines we brought.

Ingredients

6 medium Idaho potatoes, scrubbed

Olive oil

Coarse salt

Herbes de Provence

1 wedge Brie, sliced into bite-size pieces

2 avocados, sliced into bite-size pieces

Prepare the potatoes ahead of time by baking them for 40 minutes in a 300° F oven. Once they are baked almost all the way through, slice them into discs and coat the slices with olive oil, salt and herbes de Provence. Place the potatoes on the rack of a heated grill, turning them so they brown nicely. You can keep a steady stream of the grilled potatoes heading back into the kitchen where your guests are, who may assemble their own hors d'oeuvres by topping the discs with slices of Brie and avocado. Warning: These are dangerously addictive.

My Perfect Pairing: Château de Beaucastel Châteauneuf-du-Pape

From my notes: *Outrageous, delicious, the whole barnyard is here, golden hay, earthy stalls, wet horse, sweet feed, molasses; love this wine so much, at first there is black olive and truffle pizza with tomato paste and aged dry cheese*

Inspiration From My Notes: For The Love Of Basil

Today I planted my herbs. Mr. Fenner has given me the whole side garden next to my little house to work with. I only had to move a small woodpile to make the space ready for the plants. The garden store! Oh my! They have everything there. It is like a dream world of plants and flowers all come to life. I had so much fun picking out the little starts: basil, oregano, thyme, rosemary, lemon balm and mint, oh! and lavender, two kinds! I also got seeds and will try them, lettuces for a fun little edge. Mr. Fenner checked my work as I organized things. He is a good instructor and told me what would be tallest by fall, so I had the right things up front. I need a bath now. The sun is setting like a giant egg yolk into the chocolate cake dirt, and I have gritty nails and I smell good like grass and leaves and muddy spring air. The music from The Piano has been on and repeating all afternoon, it's on still. What a beautiful day. I cannot wait for the harvest.

While you may not have time (or space) for a veggie garden, herbs are effortless (and can be grown in pots taking up little room). Find your favorites already started at your garden center in spring (or any time of the year if you live in the right zone). Seeds can be finicky; easier to start with starts. Plant two of everything you like, somewhere in a convenient place in your yard or in pots on your fire escape or in your kitchen near a window. If something dies, cry only a little and do not beat yourself up (that's why you started with two of everything). Besides cooking with fresh herbs, and using them for killer cocktails (Mo-ji-tos!), their scent and presence in your space is like living near a Bordeaux bistro.

A few of my favorites: Rosemary, thyme, potted mint (which comes in many variations, such as spearmint, peppermint, chocolate mint and pineapple mint, all in my garden right now), lemon balm, sage, chives, oregano, lavender, parsley (curly and flat!). Get what you like and use it for all kinds of wonderful things inside and outside your body.

Everyday Indulgence: Savory Scones Three Ways

I love serving these flaky scones at our dinners. One of my favorite tricks is to make one full recipe but flavor it three different ways. After combining the dry ingredients and the chilled butter, I split the dough into thirds and add different herbs to each portion. They are fun to pair with a dinner that includes a few courses.

This recipe is for the basic scone mix plus what you will need to make three variations: Lavender and Sea Salt; Rosemary; Lemon Thyme and Poppy Seed.

Ingredients

2 cups spelt flour

¼ cup turbinado sugar

1 tablespoon baking powder

¾ teaspoon salt

5 tablespoons unsalted butter, very cold, sliced

1 cup heavy cream, plus more for basting

Cypress flake sea salt (for sprinkling atop scones)

To Flavor Scones Three Ways:

2 tablespoons fresh lavender, coarsely chopped (flowers or leaves)

1 ½ tablespoons fresh rosemary

3 teaspoons chopped fresh lemon thyme; 2 tablespoons poppy seeds

Preheat oven to 375° F. Sift together flour, sugar, baking powder and salt into a mixing bowl. Cut the butter into the flour mixture. If you plan to do more than one variation, this is the time to split the mixture: divide by thirds into smaller mixing bowls (about a cup of flour and butter mix per bowl for three; 1 ½ cups for two). Place the small bowls you are not ready to mix back in the icebox while you work; scones are like piecrust, they want to stay as chilly as possible while you work. Meanwhile, stir the herb addition into the first bowl and then add the cream (divide the 1 cup called for in the ingredients list into thirds or by half, if appropriate). If the dough is being picky and not gathering, add a spoonful of ice water.

Place the dough onto a floured surface and form into a nice ball, handling it as little as possible. Gently pat it into a flat round, about an inch thick. Use a big knife to quarter the round of dough for perfect portions. Place the resulting scones on an ungreased cookie sheet lined with parchment paper, and brush the tops with cream. Continue with the other portions of mix until all rounds are formed.

Just before baking, sprinkle the top of the lavender rounds and the rosemary rounds with cypress flake sea salt, and top the lemon thyme poppy seed rounds with more poppy seeds. Bake 25 minutes or so, until the tops are golden and they smell done. It will be difficult, but try to let them cool for a few minutes before serving or sampling.

My Perfect Pairing: Troon Viognier

From my notes: *Light and lifted floral, nose full of peonies and rose petals but almost creamy on the palate with pale grapefruit, chiffon flavor, bone dry and minerally*

UNEXPECTED DECADENCE

The best decadence of all may be that which surprises us. Unplanned delights often present themselves when we need them most. The trick is to be ready to receive. Watch for shooting stars, the ripple of white sails against blue skies, and perfectly wrapped boxes of chocolates which may appear suddenly on your doorstep.

Inspiration From My Notes: Preparing For Creation

Now at the easel again with lots of work ahead of me … but I'm recharged and ready. Need to get all the small pieces wrapped up for the show; we hang it Friday in Sonoma. Listening to a beautiful song mix, pale gray sky out there. This morning the boy came over and we made love before coffee. It was soft, strong, passionate and intense. Followed an emotional end to an eve last night that began up on the bluff at the beach. We went for sunset and drank a bottle of Champagne. It was unreal, so natural, so right. I love that man like no other, ever. Better paint now.

Covet energy in your life that fills you up with positivity, and watch yourself soar. Catching sunset and a taste of Champagne may help.

Everyday Indulgence: Herb Salted Figs With Honey

I regret to admit that I was well into adulthood when I met my first fresh fig. I do not, however, hold a grudge for the way it went down. There I was at a small farmer's market in Northern California on a clear, august day in very early September. I walked the lively stalls in the sea breeze with my good friend who was on her way to opening her own bona fide crêperie in a nearby town. We perused the goods and filled our sacks with market booty. At one point she squealed, "Oh! The figs are here!" and quickly bought two voluptuous boxes of the dark fruit. As we walked away, she immediately popped one into her mouth, her knees giving out in a little sway from the overwhelming pleasure on her tongue. Then she reached into the bag and suggestively fed me one of those little sacks of heaven. As I bit into the sweet, ripe flesh and experienced that luscious fruit for the first time, I was certain that virginity comes in many forms, and I could now cross figs off my list. After that, she and I wandered blissfully down the street, arm in arm, smiling wide at the blue sky and our own good fortune, enjoying multiple fig orgasms.

Ingredients

8 to 12 ripe Mission figs	Wildflower honey
Coarse salt with herbes de Provence	Almonds

There is no need to fret over fancy appetizers (or desserts) if it's fig season. Simply slice these gorgeous little flavor bombs in half lengthwise and arrange on a pretty plate. Drizzle with a touch of wildflower honey, sprinkle with your favorite coarse salt. I like sea salt with herbes de Provence, with its dried lavender and thyme, as it adds some dimension to the flavor and brings out even more of the sweetness of the figs. Serve this before dinner next to salad, alongside cheese after the main course, or with broken chunks of dark chocolate as an instant dessert. Or relish its sweet simplicity all on its own.

My Perfect Pairing: Jacques Selosse Brut Rosé NV

From my notes: *Buttered biscuits with honey, foie gras, watermelon popcorn like the one from Adrea Bachna's slumber party in fifth grade, tastes like falling in love with Indiana Jones, feels divine*

Inspiration From My Notes: Thirty-Two Robins In My Tree

There are 12 robins sitting in the tree outside my studio window. Now 16. I came up here to escape from the world. Unfortunately, I brought my phone, which of course just rang and jolted me away from here. I read my journal yesterday from 12 years ago. It was so inspiring and funny. So I am back to being conscience of and open to inspiration once again. And now, a blue sky after a downpour. The call, irrelevant and distracting, reminds me that I give too much time and energy to things that do not matter. I have come up here to sit and drink my coffee and write. (Now 18 robins in the tree.) Point is this: How can I get back to an inspirational place when the obnoxious and tedious and un-inspirational real world keeps pushing in?

What I learned by going back and reading what I wrote all those years ago was that I was not comfortable. I was quite uncomfortable. I was worried about money, sa ving for my big trip to the Netherlands, working nonstop to reach my self-imposed goal. No, I was not comfortable, but I was very ALIVE and very (20 robins in the tree now!) aware of everything around me. I felt restless and excited and like I couldn't get anything done because I wanted to do everything all at once. And then the trip and a flood of inspiration—the devotion to art and several months alone spent working, just working. Making paintings, art, writing. No sex, no boys, just me and Dutch wine made at home and virtual Vincent Van Gogh. (This bird thing is crazy out there, more are flying all around.)

Perhaps what this has made me realize is that I have always worked hard like that, and that now I am approaching a phase in my life where that work is taking over. But what about the rest of me? The other part? What about the part hungry for a diet of moody music and black coffee and new places and wild sex and fast cars and uneasy horses? I don't want to give any of that up. In fact, I want to nurture it. I am happy to have surrounded myself with people who push that in me, and I will cultivate those relationships and not take them for granted, as they keep me grounded and light as air all at once. I have to keep the connection to the magic! More witchy stuff, more mysteries! I have been solving too many mysteries lately. I will try different things, I will stretch out. I will make changes and progress. I will not sit back and relax. (Twenty-three robins are now in the tree! Are they all looking in at me?) Must remember the rides to Napa and the cherry blossoms and (25 birds now) all that love! And all that passion! And energy that can't be contained. It is still with me, but I want to touch it even more. (There are 32 robins in the tree!)

I vow to be open to the feeling I felt while riding my bicycle along the shores of the IJ near Amsterdam—where the sea grass sings actual songs if you listen and if you had a sail you wouldn't need to pedal at all.

I just went and got my camera to capture the tree full of robins. Luckily, I got several images, through the wavy old glass of the window here, catching the black-and-white moment like pale gray flowers pressed in a heavy book. Then suddenly, from nowhere and without warning, something startled them and they all flew away in one dark gray push. And then the power went out. It is raining and hailing hard.

And now it's sunny.

Expect the unexpected. No need to prepare—it's all right there with you.

Everyday Indulgence: Rustic Almond Cake

If you are looking for a sturdy little cake to dip into your Port, you just found it. This one is pretty damn good.

Ingredients

1 cup spelt flour	½ cup sugar
1 cup almond flour	2 eggs
¼ teaspoon vanilla salt	1 teaspoon vanilla extract
1 stick plus 2 tablespoons unsalted butter	1 teaspoon almond extract

Now this is easy decadence. So simple. The most difficult thing you will have to do is figure out what to serve this versatile cake with. It pairs just as well with a savory dish, like hearty lamb stew, as it does with cherry compote for an easy dessert or pretty breakfast. Plus, its prep requires only two mixing bowls and it takes only 30 minutes to bake, making it a quick fix when you need something in a hurry and don't want to mess up the kitchen before your guests arrive.

Preheat the oven to 350° F. Butter and flour an 8-inch-square pan, and set aside.

Sift all dry ingredients together—the flour, almond flour and vanilla salt. (It is a good idea to include the sifting step, as it makes for a more velvety, even cake. It only takes an extra minute.)

In another bowl, using a hand mixer, cream all the butter, the sugar, eggs and extracts. Fold the dry ingredients into the creamed sugar, and mix until incorporated, not much more. Pour it all into the pan, and bake for about 30 minutes, until a toothpick comes out clean. Enjoy this gem warm, or cooled, sliced and dipped in something deep and red (trust me, try it). Pick your poison and call me in the morning.

My Perfect Pairing: Blandy's Terrantez Madeira

From my notes: *Fedoras and mushrooms, a closet full of pelts, vodka-soaked watermelon, orange peel*

Inspiration From My Notes: Mazeppa Thoughts

Once, decades ago, I made up my mind to see a film called *Mazeppa* as a birthday gift to myself. The film was to be shown at an arthouse theater in a part of town I was unfamiliar with. Although I took one of my best girlfriends, I was terrified about the long and unfamiliar drive there. At one point, I was so unsettled I made a crazy and illegal U-turn and was immediately stopped by a police officer. I stuttered out the details of my situation, and not only did he let me go, but to my relief gave me sharp directions for getting there. I knew I had to see this film no matter what.

In a sweaty but excited state we arrived just as the lights dropped. Inside, the room smelled of dust and grade school hallways. From the opening scene, I was transported into the world of Theodore Gericault and the equestrian circus that the film centers on. I pulled paper and pen out of my little corduroy bag and in the pitch dark without ever looking down, made notes of movie lines and scribbled drawings of the dancing horses from the giant screen in front of me. A visual feast of equine anatomy, I drank those images in so deep they seared themselves into my heart and soul forever. I wanted to take this with me, wanted to be able to close my eyes and conjure *Mazeppa* scenes to play in my mind whenever I wanted. Nothing had ever spoken so closely what I felt for horses and art than that one, silky, visual song.

"To understand a horse is to flow into the slowness of her soul."

After that I looked for but could not find this film. The impact of that first viewing would feed my imagination of horses and painting for years, but I was hungry to see it again. And then, one brisk fall day as I visited friends in Nice, France, there it was. Right where it should be, in the local video shop. We all watched it together and they allowed me to rewind it a thousand times and make many more drawings and notes.

"One, two, three. One, two, three, courir au galop … I don't impose, I propose. We make love."

I own this film today, thanks to a creative and tireless search by a non-French speaking but very chivalrous lover many years later.

"He devoted his remaining days to a horse named 'my desire'."

Now I watch it with the sound shut off whenever I need to cry very hard.

Do not underestimate how far passion can take you. You can draw in the dark if you see with your soul. What does yours see now?

Everyday Indulgence: Rabbit And Plums With Syrah

What can I say about this one? It is heaven on a plate and I could eat it daily. Well, almost. Woman cannot live on rabbit alone. In fact, if you find it hard to find fresh rabbit, chicken is just as good prepared exactly the same way. If you don't have Syrah, use any other full-bodied red wine. You need a good kick from the wine to round out all the other big, deep flavors in this easy dish. So a bold red blend or Zinfandel is also good here.

Ingredients

1 rabbit, cut into pieces, or substitute whole, bone-in chicken thighs and breasts

Olive oil

1 onion, chopped

5 cloves garlic, minced, plus more if needed

Fresh rosemary

Flour, for dredging

Coarse salt and fresh pepper

1 cup dried plums, snipped in half

¾ cup dried figs, snipped in half

1 bottle full-bodied red wine

1 cup chicken stock, plus more if needed

Balsamic vinegar

Polenta (see "Divine Decadence" for recipe)

Parsley

Stop working around 3 p.m. for about 30 minutes to get this one going. Then, if you must, you can go back to the desk and finish your workday with the sweet yet invigorating scent of this rosemary-infused dish cheerfully pushing you through it. This is also a great excuse to poke your head out the door and catch some afternoon air while you snip fresh rosemary and parsley from your herb garden.

In a large skillet, put some olive oil over medium to high heat, and cook the chopped onion and minced garlic until tender. Add some coarsely chopped rosemary and let it infuse the oil. Move most of the onion, garlic and rosemary to a big stew pot, all the while inhaling deeply for the best effects of the rosemary. Salt and pepper the meat, dredge in flour, and sear it in the hot, infused oil. While it browns (I like mine really brown and sealed on the outside, the rest of the cooking will happen in the braising), snip the dried figs and plums (yes, they're prunes, but dried plums sounds much sexier!) into a big bowl and add most of the bottle of wine. Microwave the wine and plums on high for a minute or so, while also readying a cup of chicken stock for the braising pot. Keep your eye on the meat and transfer it to the braising pot as the pieces become seared all around; reserve the searing pan with its oil.

Once that is all done, cover the onions and meat with the wine and dried fruit and the stock, then add more rosemary, salt and pepper, a splash of balsamic vinegar and the reserved oil you cooked the meat in. Bring this to a soft boil. Taste the dish. (Here is a little secret. I once used a wine that was a bit too on the acidic side. To balance the flavor, I added a big tablespoon of blackberry jam. It was exactly right! You may want to add that in anyway, just for fun.) Once it comes to a boil, turn it way down and braise the meat for as long as you like, but no less than 90 minutes. See? It will be ready by 5 p.m. and you still have time to go back to the "office" and finish that proposal on your desk. Take the rest of the wine with you if you like. The recipe called for almost all of the wine for a good reason.

I love this dish with polenta prepared very clean and simply, no cheese. The final touch is fresh parsley, and curly is better for this one. Mound up the polenta, top with sauce and a generous hunk of meat, finish with chopped parsley, and prepare to enter Heaven. Good job getting that proposal in, too.

My Perfect Pairing: Penfolds Grange

From my notes: *At the start, thistle and clover, anise, black licorice; reduced, whiff of cheese, bready butter, later; the palate just woke up! explosive fruit, wow this is amazing now*

Inspiration From My Notes: Strong Women Characters

I have just come from Yvonne. It's night and I'm waiting for a tram. I feel like I must savor with every part of me what we have shared today. It was a kind of dream. It was a whole day long. I want to always remember the beautiful color of her face, her green scarf, her woolly black coat. Her short sweet curly braided hair. Her eyes deep with being soft and so well used. Her good hands. I miss her already. How can one person touch a life so deeply as she has? But I am joyful, because I think she knows about this. I feel weak with a day so full of fragility. I feel sad yet completely liberated. I want to sleep in between clean sheets and just be.

...

The words above came from my journal entry after spending a very special day with Yvonne Vera, a woman author from Zimbabwe I met during my time in Amsterdam while she was on a book tour. At the time I had shyly approached her after her reading to let her know how much I had loved hearing her words in her own lyrical voice. To my surprise and delight, she looked deeply into my eyes, and we connected, falling fast into a dreamy sisterhood of mutual admiration. We spent the next four days together, our minds intertwined like reunited soul mates, walking the city and talking incessantly. Then she left on the train for her next promotional stop. We kept in touch for several years after that, sending postcards and invitations never realized. ("Come and paint," she would write, "the African moon is good.")

Slowly, over time and busy-ness, we slipped apart. When I sat down to create this book, I found a photo of the two of us tucked into one of my journals. Curious about her current life, I looked her up. It had been a few years since I had heard from her. A sharp sadness shook me hard and fast when my online search turned up results that included a reference not only to her birth date, but to the date of her death as well. She had passed away a few years ago at just over 40. Tears burned my cheeks, and at that moment, the true meaning of this book was driven home in a hard and real way: Life. Is. Short.

Reflecting on your day for even a few moments is a great way to remember experiences and to process what happened beyond the endless lists you keep of all things practical. Who or what really touched you, and in what way? How did it taste? What will you remember about it when they are gone forever?

In that vein, the final perfect pairing in this book, the T-Vine Monte Rosso Sonoma Cabernet, deserves a few extra words, in homage to an insight on the part of its maker, the late Greg Brown. His words spoke to me and will, I think, speak to many of you as well. Reflecting on the wine he'd had the honor to make from the legendary vineyard, Greg said, "I hope wine lovers take the opportunity to experience a dream that manifested into a bottle of art. It's like a fantasy that juices up your life and inspires you towards stepping outside your perception of reality. It inspires me."

This is exactly what I believe wine is. Bottles of art. Bottles of life. Bottles to inspire life.

My Perfect Pairing: T-Vine Monte Rosso Sonoma Cabernet

From my notes: *Candied flowers, structured base layered up with dense fruit, punchy tannins promising lots of hot nights to come (in a year's time?); really good! Later: orange marmalade on a chocolate graham cracker*

UNEXPECTED DECADENCE

AFTERWORD

I don't know if it is the result of digging into all these years of struggle, hope, creation—searching, joy, celebration, fear, and evolution—but I'm sitting here now listening to inspiring music and I'm just overwhelmed by the magnificence of being aware of all these crazy days of my life. I have been brave and awake and it has been worth every minute. I am so lucky, so happy, so fulfilled. Realizing how hard, how simple, how profound my journey has been. I am so blessed to live this life. Thanks to the Universe and all that IS—thanks to the gift of blessings so large I will never know their edges, their end. Truly I have found my wide-eyed bliss. I feel so unbelievably lucky. I promise not to take any of it for granted and to give back the gift tenfold. I promise to keep my awareness wildly awake and tender, like the countless emerald leaves trembling in the wind surrounding the ponyfields of my days. I vow to always acknowledge with gratitude the ever-present comfort of the silver moon in all her phases—singing her silent songs to me each night—as she spins a velvet soundtrack for all my dreams to come.

Coudoulet de Beaucastel Côte du Rhône
Mourvèdre, Grenache, Cinsault, Syrah
(B) baked ham w/ pineapple & cherry
(P) ladybugs
floral big light ness - meadow air
in olive - cool

NOTES

NOTES

NOTES